SHA-MANIC PLAYS

**QUEEN MARGARET COLLEGE
CORSTORPHINE CAMPUS LIBRARY**

―――

Please return book by date stamped below

John Constable

SHA-MANIC PLAYS

BLACK MAS
DEAD MAN'S HANDLE
ICEMAN
THE FALSE HAIRPIECE

First published in 1997 by Oberon Books Ltd (incorporating Absolute Classics), 521 Caledonian Road, London N7 RH. Tel: 0171 607 3637/ Fax: 0171 607 3629.

British Library Cataloguing-in-Publication Data
A catalogue record for this book is available from the British Library

ISBN 1 870259 90 4

Cover design: Andrzej Klimowski

Cover typography: Richard Doust

Printed by Arrowhead Books Limited, Reading

For

Katie Nicholls

with thanks to

Di Sherlock
Gary Carter
James Richmond
The McKees

CONTENTS

PREFACE

A critic once complained that "Constable doesn't tell the audience what to think." Seems to me there's no shortage of Popes, Ayatollahs, politicians and other Know-Alls telling us what to think. The playwright's task is not to provide facile answers, but to ask questions, invite audiences to think for themselves. I don't want to hear my characters repeating what I already know – I want them to surprise me with things I don't know. So I'm not about to tell you how to read these plays, but I can say how they came to be written.

I owe my first play to the island and people of Trinidad. I went looking for a party and found Anancy. Blew all my money. Got a job – demolishing Lennox Raphael's firebombed theatre. Lennox encouraged me to write a play about my experiences as a white man in Carnival.

So... sooner or later a writer has to deliver – and it helps to have a deadline. I decided that if I hadn't written the play by the time I was thirty I was going to have to top myself. It did the trick – I finished it the day before my thirtieth birthday. It then sat (unread) at the Royal Court for more than a year before I bumped into the Trinidadian playwright, Mustapha Matura, who read it, liked it and arranged a reading within a week.

Black Mas is not about black culture but white people's fears, fantasies and sneaking envy of its life-affirming energy. The wit and rhythm of Trinidadian patois helped free up my own voice. I tried to evoke the Carnival misrule that heightens, ritualises and releases racial and sexual tensions, the sense of myth and magic invading our everyday lives. The play personifies this Dionysian spirit of Carnival as Anancy – the Spider who tricked Death in the African folk-tale – morally ambivalent, socially disruptive, trickster god of change and violent revelation.

In the Anancy stories, Spider's witness is Broken Wing, John Crow, a shady character who shows up in various guises in much of my recent work. *The False Hairpiece* has the manic depressive son, Jake, hell-bent on solving the riddle of his father's death. Jake Crow was first conceived as an avenging angel returned to haunt his guilt-stricken family. In writing the play I discovered that this is indeed the family's expectation, but that Jake himself has no interest in retribution – he's come home determined to "heal the rift". Unfortunately, his good intentions wreak havoc on a family sunk deep in denial.

As someone whose world-view was radically altered by experiments with sacramental chemicals, I am naturally inclined to see the so-called War On Drugs as an integral part of the so-called Drug Problem. I didn't want to preach so I wrote *Iceman* – a black farce in which the psychic trousers keep falling down. Here, Crowe is an undercover cop who sacrifices his identity, moral authority and ultimately his sanity, in a drug-fuelled bid to crack his own case.

The inner life again collides with external reality in my short play, *Dead Man's Handle*, where a man in a coma journeys through an interior landscape in search of a death he can get to grips with.

These are plays about identity and the quest to validate experience. I don't deny the importance of the day-to-day struggle to survive, but I am more interested in the extremes of human behaviour, where characters push themselves to the edge, confronting their own deaths in order to live.

Writing a play is a journey of discovery, a springboard for the leap into the Unknown. I'm not the Priest telling you what to believe. It's just John Crow up to his old shamanic tricks, naming his demons to be free from fear, hunting for visions, riddles, songs, stories, keys to unlock the mystery. The words are not there to "pin it down", but to open it all up and let "it" take flight.

John Constable
London, 1997

BLACK MAS

CHARACTERS

ROSE LORRAINE
A charismatic English singer, on holiday in Trinidad.

JIMMY
Her lover and manager, a sassy, street-wise white boy.

ROY
A black Trinidadian hotel-keeper, masquerading as SPIDER.

PETER MARDUKE
A wealthy, white Trinidadian, masquerading as DEATH.

MONKEY MAN
An unidentified masquerader.

The action takes place in the Hotel Thread, Port of Spain, Trinidad, at the height of Carnival between midnight and 2 am. Tuesday February 23rd 1982. A three day non-stop party is nearing its climax.

Sound: Calypso, Soca and Steelband music. The amplification source is located offstage to create the effect of the music playing in the street (The play was written with the music of the 1982 Carnival in mind). The onstage radio has its own speaker.

Language: ROY and MARDUKE speak the Trinidadian dialect (although MARDUKE occasionally slips into a more formal English). JIMMY and ROSE have learned to imitate the dialect.

Black Mas was first performed by Foco Novo, directed by Roland Rees, with the following cast:

ROSE LORRAINE, Carole Harrison

JIMMY, Ian Reddington

ROY, Trevor Butler

PETER MARDUKE, James Snell

Designed by Peter Whiteman.

Costumes by Sheelagh Killeen.

Soca music rapidly growing louder. Lights fade up on the empty lobby of the Hotel Thread, a cheap boarding house in Port of Spain, Trinidad. Upstage left: a door leading to the street. Above the door, a sign: HOTEL THREAD, printed in reverse letters on glass. Upstage centre: the reception desk/bar, and a doorway leading to the hotel interior. On the desk: a bell, a radio and a folded newspaper. A poster on the wall reads: DIS YEAR PLAY MAS - AFRICAN MYTHS AND LEGENDS. In front of the desk: two barstools. Upstage right: a bedroom, a white gauze box containing a bed. The voices of JIMMY and ROSE are heard from the street, arguing with a silent and invisible third party.

JIMMY: Now come on, bro'. Take it easy. Let's stay cool tonight, huh?

ROSE: Just fuck off will you! I don't care if you're black white yellow or blue. I'm sick and tired of being hustled. Okay?

JIMMY: Come on, Rose. The guy's drunk.

ROSE: Look, mister, why don't you go fuck a chicken?

JIMMY: Shut up, Rose! Hey! Back off, man! That's my lady you're messing with. Rose! Get inside! Go on!

ROSE: We're going in here?

JIMMY: For fuck's sake don't argue, woman! Come on!

The street door flies open with a loud burst of music. JIMMY pushes ROSE into the room, slams the door behind them, leans back against it with a sigh of relief. ROSE wears a chic micro-skirt over tights and a skin-tight vest that leaves little to the imagination. Her make-up completes a look of elegant eroticism, now slightly dishevelled. JIMMY wears a "Black Power" T-shirt and jeans. The music gradually fades away.

ROSE: It's always the same with you. You let yourself get drawn in and then you panic at the last moment.

JIMMY: I did not panic! You were the one who couldn't handle it.

ROSE: Oh come on, Jimmy. Don't just throw it back at me.

JIMMY: Anyway, what the hell do you expect slap bang in the middle of Carnival?

ROSE: Well for one thing, I expect you to look after me a bit better.

JIMMY: And what is that supposed to mean?

ROSE: It means you should stay awake when we're dancing in the middle of a big crowd. That scene out there could've turned very nasty.

JIMMY: Look, if I'd picked a fight with every guy who tried to stick his hand up your skirt, we'd never've made it in one piece. That crowd could've eaten us alive. Face it, Rose. Those streets are out of control. The only thing you can do is go with it. It's madness to resist.

ROSE: I can't stand crowds like that... Like that night in Chicago when the audience rushed the stage...

JIMMY: Now that was what I call dangerous.

ROSE: But at least that was my audience. I know how to control them...

JIMMY rings the desk bell.

So what are we doing now?

JIMMY: Right now you need to chill out, sweetheart. You were coming on really heavy with that guy out there. I'm going to try and get us a room for the night.

ROSE: Here? Bit sleazy, isn't it?

JIMMY: (*Reads the Hotel sign, amused.*) Hotel Thread, Madame.

ROSE: Hotel Dread, more like! What a dump!

JIMMY: Liz Taylor, I can do without.

ROSE: Bette Davis. Christ, Jimmy, you really do pick
them. First the shanty town and now this. The original
no-holds-barred Adventure Holiday!

She surveys the room with distaste.

It's probably a bordello. I ask you, Jimmy, what sort
of a person calls his place Hotel Thread?

JIMMY: A tailor?

ROSE: What's the time?

JIMMY: (*Checks his watch.*) It's past midnight. If you
want we can take a taxi back to Laventille.

ROSE: And scramble up that hill in the dark? With God
knows how many horny black guys lurking in the bushes.

JIMMY: Alright. Then we stay here.

*JIMMY rings the bell. ROSE walks over to the rocking chair,
sets it rocking.*

ROSE: This is really the pits!

JIMMY: Don't go bitching to me, love. As far as I'm
concerned there's a party going on outside, and
we're missing it.

ROSE: I'm sorry to be such a drag, Jimmy. I'm sure
you'd be having a much better time without me.

JIMMY: I never said that.

Pause. Soca music off.

ROSE: Well where are they then, the contacts, the
music scene connections? That's your fucking job,
remember? Right now we could be in one of those

big Maraval house parties, drinking rum and coke with the Calypsonians. When Mick Jagger came to Trinidad, I bet he didn't stay in a shitty joint like this.

JIMMY: You fucking little primadonna! If you wanted the Holiday Inn, why didn't you say so? We can afford it. It was you kept going on about the fucking action... "I wanna go Street..."

ROSE: When I said street, I didn't mean that street! And I certainly didn't mean Laventille Hill! I didn't mean we had to squat in a corrugated iron shack with nowhere to wash.

JIMMY: Okay, I know it was a bit basic.

ROSE: And the rats, Jimmy! I don't know how you could sleep with rats scuttling under the bed and God knows what monster bugs crawling in the shadows.

JIMMY: You've been spoiled, love. It doesn't hurt to take a look at life in the raw...

ROSE: Hey! What is this? Third world crash-course for poor little white girl? What do I have to do? Catch yellow fever from an open cesspit? Get gang-banged by the Desperados Steelband? Come on! Tell me! Huh!

JIMMY: Look, all the time we were staying up there we didn't have one really heavy scene. Right? And we got to see some of the real Trinidad, not just the tourist brochure. I know it's harder for a woman to deal with head-on...

ROSE laughs.

But those guys are pretty cool really. It's Carnival. They're just looking for a good time.

ROSE: And I'm the white woman on the hill who's gonna give it to them?

JIMMY: Well maybe that's your secret fantasy.

ROSE: Oh yeah!

JIMMY: Well you keep going on about it.

ROSE: Well if it was all so hunky dory happy families up there, how come you were sleeping with a bread knife under your pillow?

JIMMY: I thought it would make you feel more secure.

ROSE: I didn't know whether to be more afraid of them breaking in to rape me or you slashing away with your carving knife.

JIMMY: All right. Go on. Laugh. But I tell you Rose, there's more real life up on Laventille Hill...

ROSE: Yeah! Rats, cockroaches, crazy dogs...

JIMMY: Than in all your Hiltons and Holiday Inns in the whole fucking western world! They're all the same those places, wherever you go. Sunburnt white money, playing it safe. You come to Trinidad for that? For Carnival?

ROSE: I don't need a lecture on Street from you. And I never said I wanted the Hilton.

JIMMY: So quit bitching about Laventille. Tonight we stay here. Tomorrow we look for something better. OK?

ROSE: I guess anything's better than walking up that hill in the dark. If we can get a room. Doesn't look like there's anybody here.

JIMMY: There must be.

He rings the bell repeatedly.

Tomorrow afternoon we can pick up the luggage.

ROSE: If it's still there.

They laugh resignedly, somewhat reconciled.

JIMMY: At least we stashed the money.

ROSE: You're right, Jimmy. I'll feel better after a lie down. I just need a good night's sleep.

JIMMY: It's all right, darlin'. I understand.

They embrace. Enter ROY, the desk clerk, through the interior door. He is Afro-Trinidadian, very relaxed, wearing smart casual shirt and pants. His entrance catches JIMMY and ROSE by surprise.

ROY: Wha' happenin'? I see yuh all enjoyin' Carnival.

JIMMY: Yeah, we're having a wild time.

ROY: Is de wildest night tonight, boy. Dem go dance 'til dey drop. Yuh ain't see nuttin' like dis in de whole wide world. Not Rio. Not New Orleans. Dis is de big one.

JIMMY: I believe you, man. We've been in the streets since early morning. It's been one crazy scene after another.

ROY: Yuh play Mas?

JIMMY: No. We didn't have any costumes. We dressed up for J'ouvert in some old sheets yesterday morning.

ROY: Yuh must come back next year an' play Mas. Yuh go join up wid a Mas camp, dey givin' yuh Mas an' all. And how's m'lady?

ROSE: I'm just about ready to drop.

ROY: So wha' happenin'? Yuh lookin' for a room?

JIMMY: That's right.

ROY: Yuh does pick a great time to be lookin' for a room I must say. Some ah dem guesthouse does book out month ahead yuh know.

ROSE: Yeah, we found out the hard way.

ROY: Well I tell yuh, yuh is lucky, lady. It have a German couple leave here only last night. Can't stand de pace. Dey take de night-ferry to Tobago.

JIMMY: Great. How much for one night?

ROY: Thirty dollar.

JIMMY: Trinidad dollars?

ROY: Yuh foolin' wi' me? Carnival rate is all Yankee dollar. Thirty dollar US is sixty TT. Is de cheapest yuh find anywhere in town, if yuh find anyting at all tonight.

JIMMY: Okay, man, it's late. I'm not going to argue. Here you go...

He takes out his wallet, gives ROY the money.

ROY: Ain' no sense worryin' over money in Carnival, boy. How much yuh have, yuh go lose it all one way or another.

He picks up the folded newspaper, swats a fly.

Damn flies! T'ain' natural so early in de year. Yuh ain' have no luggage or nuttin'?

JIMMY: We've been staying with friends up in Laventille. We left all our stuff with them.

ROY: Whoo! Up in de shanty town! You was livin' in a shack?

ROSE: That's right.

ROY: Dat's what called "visitin' de natives". So why yuh don't go sleep dere? Yuh 'fraid to walk up de hill?

JIMMY: No, we just felt like being in town for the big night. We might go out again later.

ROY: Well I don' blame yuh if yuh 'fraid to walk yuh
    lady up dere, boy. It have some BAD johns in
    Laventille!

ROSE: Can we see the room, please. I want to lie down.

ROY: No problem. I tell yuh sometin' for nuttin'.

ROSE: Yeah?

ROY: Don' trust nobody.

ROSE: Does that include you?

ROY: (*Laughs.*) Yuh is quick, lady! Here...

He shows them the bedroom. JIMMY and ROSE enter
through a slit in the gauze. Lights up in the bedroom.
ROSE lies down on the bed. JIMMY massages her. ROY
returns to his desk, switches on the radio, picks up his
newspaper. The bedroom and lobby scenes are played
simultaneously, the focus shifting from one to the other.
JIMMY and ROSE can hear (but not see) what's
happening in the lobby. Likewise ROY can hear what's
happening in the bedroom.

RADIO VOICE: (*American Evangelist, deep South.*) That's
    right! THERE IS POWER IN THE BLOOD! The
    blood of our Lord and Saviour Jesus Christ is like an
    open ticket on a Direct Express Train to GOD! So the
    first thing you gotta ask yourself is: "Do I have a
    ticket?" Because you don't get on without a ticket.
    There's no Free Rides on this train! You know, one
    time a few years back, I was waiting for a train at a
    small country station in the mid-west of the United
    States, when I noticed this dog tied up to a wall.
    There was a sign on the wall, and the sign said:
    "Lost Property". Now that dog was shivering and
    whining and looking real sorry for himself. So I
    went and asked the Station Master: "What's the
    matter with that dog?" And the man answered me,

he said: "I don't know where the dog's going. Dog don't know where he's going. And dog done chewed up his own despatch label."

ROY switches off the radio, reads his newspaper. JIMMY is getting turned on by ROSE, his massage now unmistakeably erotic. ROSE abruptly sits up in bed.

ROSE: Not now, Jimmy! Please...

JIMMY: What's the matter?

ROSE: I can't... I'm too tense.

JIMMY: You don't have to do anything. Just relax and let me do everything.

ROSE: Oh Jimmy, you don't understand. You can't understand the strain I'm under.

JIMMY: Thought you'd enjoy being the centre of attention and all.

ROSE: I don't enjoy you having to protect me every time I step out on the street. It's so fucking macho, this culture.

JIMMY: How do you think I feel? Always having to keep one eye on you like you're my wife or something. I could've had fun with some of those sexy black girls. I only stuck with you because you wanted me to.

ROSE: And then I don't even do a wife's duty, don't even give you a decent screw.

JIMMY: Rose...

ROSE: Or would you prefer a blow-job?

JIMMY: For Christ's sake! Keep your voice down.

ROSE: Well? You're hardly sensitive to my feelings at the moment. Don't you understand, Jimmy? All day long I've been ogled and groped by hundreds of faceless men in crowds. I'm starting to feel like an inflatable sex doll.

JIMMY: You're so melodramatic.

ROSE: Horny men are so impersonal. Fuck anything with tits and ass.

JIMMY: Don't mind me. I'm just the fucking manager.

ROSE: I don't mean it like that, Jimmy. It's not you. It's just... Well this isn't exactly my idea of a romantic holiday, you know.

JIMMY: I didn't know what to expect either. But I do wish you'd quit playing the little lost innocent.

ROSE: What kind of sly dig is that?

JIMMY: Come on, Rosie! Your whole stage act is set up to turn on the boys.

ROSE: They do come to hear me sing too, you know.

JIMMY: They come to see you come, baby. To see you shake your tits and bump your beautiful ass.

ROSE: If that's all you see in me, you better find yourself another act, mister!

She turns away from him. Pause. ROY sees a fly on the desk. Folds the newspaper. Swats it.

JIMMY: Hey, come on, little star. I was only joking. Anyway, it's no sin to be sexy.

ROSE: Jimmy...

JIMMY: Yeah?

ROSE: Why don't we split to Tobago right after Carnival? Treat ourselves to a real tourist beach holiday.

JIMMY: Sure. Why not?

ROSE: Just swim and lie in the sun and relax.

JIMMY: That's right, angel. Relax.

He kisses her neck. She breaks away again.

ROSE: Jimmy! Please. Don't hustle me. I've been
   hustled quite enough for one night already. It's so hot
   and sticky. I can't breathe!

JIMMY: We are almost on the equator.

ROSE: And there's no privacy.

JIMMY: Why are you talking so fucking loud, then?

*They whisper. Steelband music off, louder as the street
door opens. Enter MARDUKE, masquerading as
DEATH, stealthily closing the door behind him. He wears
black gloves and bodystocking painted with white bones to
create a walking skeleton effect, white Death mask and
black top hat. He holds up his doctor's bag, striking a
pose.*

ROY: (*Glances up warily from his newspaper, speaking in a
   spooky neutral voice, to audience.*) Anancy come to de
   river. Anancy he say: "Tomorrow same time, yuh go
   burst yuh banks. Yuh hear? Yuh go flood all de
   earth!"

DEATH moves towards the desk, menacing.

Anancy come to de anthill. Anancy tell de ant:
"Tomorrow same time, yuh all go come here. Yuh
hear? I go give yuh someting to eat."

*DEATH raises his top hat to ROY, who looks hard at
him, his face creasing to a smile.*

Mistah Marduke!

He laughs heartily, banging on the desk.

Wha' happenin', sah?

MARDUKE removes the Death mask, puts it on the desk. He is a white Trinidadian. He takes off his right hand glove, offers ROY his hand.

MARDUKE: Yuh is de first dat spotted me, Roy. Put it dere, bro'!

They exchange a soul handshake.

ROY: Yuh don' fool me, sah, no matter how much yuh trick yuhself up! Is someting in de way yuh move.

MARDUKE: Oh yeah? How yuh mean, Roy?

ROY: (*Rubs his chin.*) Well now dat hard to say, boy... Maybe is de feelin' like yuh checkin' everyting out before yuh make yuh move. Yuh dig?

MARDUKE: Roy, yuh talkin' through yuh ass again, boy!

He laughs, takes off the other glove, sits to take off his shoes.

ROY: So what yuh doin' here dis time ah night?

MARDUKE: I come in to change me Mas. It have some wild woman on de street tonight. Got to look me best, right?

MARDUKE opens the doctor's bag. During the following conversation he takes out shirt and trousers, puts them on. Puts gloves and Death mask carefully back in the bag. Puts on his shoes. Tousles his hair to complete his transformation to casual elegance.

ROY: True. Yuh ain' have much luck wid de ladies got up like dat.

MARDUKE: Don' worry 'bout me, boy. I can strip for action in twenty second when de goin' get hot. I go keep it on underneath, see, like Clark Kent...

ROY: Superman...

MARDUKE: Right. Any man make me vex tonight, I go put de fear ah God into he.

ROY: Better take it easy tonight, boy. Yuh know dey say two ting Trinidadian fear is rain and a white man.

MARDUKE: Well I tell you, Roy, all day and all night I jammin' in de street, ain' nobody know if I black or white. I tell yuh, Roy, de Great Leveller.

ROY: True. People is people when it come to Death.

MARDUKE: I ain' have no hustle, de whole day and night! I tell yuh I feelin' totally safe out dere.

ROY: Well yuh know, Mistah Marduke, de safest place to be is in de eye of de storm.

Storyteller voice.

It have two monkey, one name Donaxmenuttin', de other name Trouble. Dem playin' hide and seek. Donaxmenuttin' go hide in de long grass. Soon de Sheriff come along and he say: "What yuh name, boy?" Donaxmenuttin' say: "Donaxmenuttin'." Sheriff say: "Yuh lookin' for trouble, boy?" Donaxmenuttin' say: "No. Trouble lookin' for me."

MARDUKE: (*Laughs.*) Good one, Roy! So what happenin' with you?

ROY: Fly on yuh shirt, sah.

He brushes it away.

Here is quiet as de grave. I come back half hour ago, de whole place empty. Only it have two crazy white people check in here.

MARDUKE: Oh yeah? Tourist?

ROY: Dem come in here, after midnight on a Carnival Monday! No luggage or nuttin'.

MARDUKE: Dey lookin' for a room?

ROY: I tink dey lookin' for a place to cool out. English couple. A funky white boy wid he foxy lady.

MARDUKE: She someting?

ROY: (*Draws closer to MARDUKE, lowering his voice conspiratorially.*) Whoo! Man, she hot! She look like she all ready to bust into flame I tell yuh!

MARDUKE: Just need de match to set she alight, eh Roy?

ROY: Man, she need a candle, I tellin' you!

ROSE sits up suddenly, with a suppressed scream.

ROSE: Jimmy! Jimmy! A spider!

JIMMY: Where?

ROSE: Look! On the wall! Oh God it's huge! Jimmy, get rid of it.

ROY jerks his head in the direction of the bedroom. He and MARDUKE listen, exchanging amused looks.

JIMMY: It's not doing you any harm. It's just sitting there on the wall.

ROSE: It's watching me. I know the minute I take my eyes off it, it's going to come and crawl all over me.

JIMMY: Oh come on, Rose, for God's sake!

ROSE: It's probably poisonous. It looks poisonous.

JIMMY: I'm sure it's quite harmless.

ROSE: Jimmy, please. Get rid of it.

JIMMY: (*Sighs.*) All right. I'll get rid of it.

JIMMY sits on the side of the bed, takes off one shoe, gets up and moves towards the spider, the shoe ready to strike.

Suddenly, the spider runs down the wall and under the bed.

ROSE: (*Jumps.*) Oh my God, it's under the bed!

JIMMY: Well get off the fucking bed then!

ROSE: (*Jumping off the bed.*) Jimmy you are fucking useless sometimes!

JIMMY: What? You saw how fast he moved.

ROSE: I'm going out to the lobby. And I'm not sleeping in this room with that spider!

She leaves the bedroom.

JIMMY: Fuck you, Rose!

He gets down on his hands and knees, his shoe in his hand, peering under the bed. ROSE walks over to join MARDUKE and ROY at the desk.

ROSE: Hi!

MARDUKE: Hello there, beautiful. How are you dis strange and shiftin' night?

ROSE: I'm fine.

ROY: Yuh don't look fine. Yuh lookin' good, girl!

They laugh.

Yuh done with yuh restin'? I done tell yuh quick.

ROSE, momentarily confused, looks at MARDUKE.

MARDUKE: (*Offering his hand.*) Peter... Peter Marduke.

ROSE: (*Taking his hand.*) Rose Lorraine.

MARDUKE: Rose Lorraine... That's a pretty name.

ROSE: I know. I made it up myself.

MARDUKE looks puzzled.

It's my stage name. I'm a singer.

MARDUKE: No kiddin'!

ROSE: 'Voodoo Radio'? Number three in the U.S. charts.

Off their blank grins.

You mean you haven't heard of me?

MARDUKE: Can't say I have.

ROSE: You will. Rose Lorraine. I'm going to be big.

MARDUKE: (*Laughs.*) Well, well... Yuh hear dat, Roy? We in luck tonight. A beautiful and talented English Rose in town for Carnival! We better make sure she well looked after.

ROY: True, Miss. Yuh must let Mistah Marduke show yuh around and all.

JIMMY bangs under the bed with his shoe, bangs his head on the underside of the bed. ROSE pointedly ignores the noises off.

JIMMY: Shit!

ROSE: How long have you lived here?

MARDUKE: I's a Trini born and bred, lady. Right, Roy?

ROY: True.

MARDUKE: I know me way around. You want something to drink?

ROSE: That's exactly what I need.

MARDUKE: Rum and coca cola?

ROSE: Perfect.

MARDUKE: Roy boy, gi' we bottle rum and a bottle coke wid plenty crush ice.

He takes out money, slaps it on the desk. ROY produces three glasses from under the desk, mixes rum and cokes. MARDUKE opens a silver cigarette case, offers ROSE a cigarette.

MARDUKE: Smoke?

ROSE: Thanks.

She takes a cigarette. MARDUKE lights it and his own cigarette. Meanwhile, back in the bedroom, JIMMY starts rolling a spliff. He can hear but not see what's happening in the lobby.

MARDUKE: Yes, we've had one or two rock stars visit us for Carnival. Mick Jagger was here a couple of times you know.

ROSE: So I heard...

MARDUKE: Yes, I took him round, introduced him to our local artists and musicians, showed him the night-life. You don't really see Trinidad unless you have someone to show you round.

ROSE: Any place is the right place if you have the right connections.

MARDUKE: Dig it!

ROY: So what kind ah music yuh playin'?

ROSE: I don't really fit into any category. I'm into fusions, you know? Musical cocktails... Three parts psychedelic soul to one part reggae with a shot of latin rhythm on the rocks.

MARDUKE: Shaken not stirred.

ROSE: (*Laughing.*) You got it! Last Tango in the Nightclub at the End of Time. Yeah... I pick up on all kinds of influences. That's what I'm doing here.

ROY: Lookin' for yuh roots?

ROSE: It's all here, in this incredible melting pot. You got the European, the Indian, the Chinese... You listen to these Calypsos, you got American Soul and Salsa mixed into Soca Tempo... And it's all rooted in African drums, tribal dances, trance dances, women stomping the earth all night long...

ROY: (*Laughing.*) Yuh lookin' for voodoo, Miss, yuh go up in de hills on a full moon...

MARDUKE: Don' yuh believe dat nonsense.

ROSE: Oh I know a lot of it's superstition but... well maybe I'm a natural believer. Like when I'm on stage... It's like I tune into something that like sings and dances through me. You know what I mean?

ROY: (*Handing out drinks.*) Whoo! Yuh is right, Mistah Marduke.

MARDUKE: Ain' she someting, Roy? Cheers!

MARDUKE, ROSE and ROY chink glasses, drink.

ROY: Yuh should introduce Miss Rose to some ah dem Calypsonians.

ROSE: Yeah! I'd love to meet those guys.

MARDUKE: If we'd met earlier, I could've taken you round the Calypso tents. After Carnival I'll introduce you to Sparrow.

ROSE: You know Sparrow?

MARDUKE: Like de back of me hand, girl!

ROY: Mistah Marduke is quite a celebrity heself in Port ah Spain, Miss. He one of de richest men on de island.

MARDUKE: My father's the one who owns it all actually. But I tell yuh, Roy, if I take Rose to meet dem Calypsonians, I better look out for she.

ROY: True. It have some BAD black man when it come to a pretty girl like Miss Rose, no offence sah!

JIMMY comes out of the bedroom.

MARDUKE: Watch out, Roy! Here come de Sheriff!

ROSE and MARDUKE have taken the two barstools. JIMMY has to stand.

ROSE: Oh! Peter, this is Jimmy...

MARDUKE: (*Offers his hand.*) Peter Marduke.

JIMMY shakes his hand.

I was just saying to Rose here, you never know who you'll run into in Carnival. When I dropped in to check out Roy just now, I didn't expect we'd have company.

JIMMY: Tell me about it! Ever since we got here it's been one non-stop chance encounter that's led us to places you wouldn't believe!

They laugh.

ROSE: Did you get it?

JIMMY: No, It got away.

MARDUKE: Get what?

ROSE: A spider. In the bedroom. It looked like a Tarantula or something.

She shivers involuntarily.

ROY: Yuh 'fraid of an itsy bitsy spider, Miss? Spider don' do yuh no harm if yuh leave he alone. We ain' have so much ah dem poison spider down here.

MARDUKE: Hey, Roy, fix Jimmy a drink will yuh?

ROY: It all in de mind, girl.

He fixes JIMMY a rum and coke.

MARDUKE: Yuh just here for holiday?

JIMMY: We're here for the whole trip, man. You know? Looking for a slice of the action.

MARDUKE: So yuh tink to crash de wildest party in de world?

JIMMY: Who's talking about crashing? There's no formal invitations I've heard of.

ROY: (*Gives JIMMY his drink.*) Yuh feel to free up, no?

JIMMY: True. I feelin' free, brother.

MARDUKE: Hey, Roy, he talkin' like a real Trini.

ROY: True, yuh learn fast, boy. If yuh lookin' to party, yuh come to de right place. De biggest bacchanal is a Trinidad Carnival.

JIMMY: Right!

JIMMY and ROY chink glasses.

MARDUKE: So here's to the whole trip, Jimmy.

JIMMY: I'll drink to that.

They all chink glasses.

ROY: I tell yuh, yuh can do anyting yuh want. Yuh can lie down and roll on yuh back in de street if yuh want.

JIMMY: You said it man! Some of those scenes out there are so weird. I kept doing double-takes. You know? "Jimmy, man, you're hallucinating."

ROY: Tonight de night yuh fantasy reality, yuh dig?

ROSE: All I can say is you people got yourselves some real freaky feathered fantasies coming true tonight! One minute you're in a crowd of dancing Mayan Gods and Demons, the next you're facing up to a battalion of Swapo guerrillas!

JIMMY: There was even a guy dressed up as a walking skeleton.

MARDUKE: Yuh was 'fraid?

JIMMY: Nah! He scared the life out of Rose though.

ROSE: He did not!

ROY: What he do?

ROSE: What do you think! He grabbed hold of me from behind.

ROY: Ah, he jammin' wid yuh. Yuh don' like dat?

ROSE: I was getting sick and tired of guys rubbing themselves up against me, especially when you can't even see who they are.

ROY: True. Is terrible de ting a man get up to when yuh ain' see he face. Right, Mistah Marduke?

MARDUKE: True, Roy. (*To ROSE.*) Yuh see Minshall's band?

ROSE: The butterflies? Beautiful!

ROY: Dat man have tree thousand butterfly in de street tonight. Everyting from de Wings ah Sin to de Butterfly ah Death.

JIMMY: I liked that Marilyn Monroe.

MARDUKE: It have a sexy black queen wearin' dat blonde beauty, eh Jimmy?

JIMMY: She looked good, man.

ROSE: What about "The Sacred and the Profane"?

ROY: Dat is a real butterfly King for de ladies, eh Miss Rose?

ROSE: You're not kidding. The women went crazy when he came on stage at the Savannah. Guy's got a beautiful body.

ROY: Peter Samuel. Is de fourth time he win de competition: de King ah Carnival.

JIMMY: Don't forget Che Guevara, and Muhammad Ali…

MARDUKE: And de Ayatollah wid he skull face…

They're starting to get drunk, loosening up, laughing as they recall the Carnival scenes.

ROY: Dat man Minshall put de whole mad world in wings I tell yuh.

MARDUKE: You should see the work that goes into just one of those butterflies. They have to staple on thousands of sequins to make up a single face.

ROSE: I'd love to have visited the Mas camps.

ROY: Who yuh rate to win de Road March, Marduke?

MARDUKE: Well I reckon it have to be "Deputy", Roy. All ah dem man and woman in town tonight, all ah dem singin': "Ah Deputy Essential".

"Deputy" is Trinidadian slang for a lover "on the side". MARDUKE says this line looking at ROSE, sharing his joke with ROY.

JIMMY: Penguin, right?

MARDUKE: Dat right, boy. Penguin sing dat song. He go win de Road March wid dat song, as I explain to Roy here.

ROSE: Peter wants to take me to meet Sparrow.

JIMMY: Sparrow the Calypsonian? Nice one, Rose.

MARDUKE: Yuh ain' married?

ROSE: No. Jimmy and I are just good friends.

JIMMY: As they say in the fanzines.

He and ROSE exchange edgy looks.

MARDUKE: So what else do you do, Jimmy?

JIMMY: I'm Rose's manager, among other things.

MARDUKE: Yuh try to manage she? Yuh got yuh work cut out for yuh dere, boy!

ROY: True. Yuh better hold onto she, when she jammin' in de street.

ROY and MARDUKE laugh.

JIMMY: I watch her, don't you worry.

MARDUKE: Don' yuh watch and worry she too much I tell yuh, or she ain' have no fun!

JIMMY: Marduke... Where have I heard that name before?

MARDUKE: How's yuh Babylonian Mythology?

JIMMY: Huh?

MARDUKE: Bel-Marduk, de All Mighty God of Babylon. He de biggest hardest meanest warrior god around, yuh dig. De story go how de Great Mother get vex and give birth to all kind ah monster. All de gods 'fraid, so dey send for MarDuk: "Hey, man, do something, 'fore yuh mudder monster go swallow we up." Now dis MarDuk he smart. He say: "Well, boys, I go get yuh out ah dis mess, yuh all know who is de Number One around here, right?"

ROSE: The gods had to make MarDuk the Big Boss.

MARDUKE: Right, and den he go mash up de monster.

ROSE: Does it run in the family?

MARDUKE: What?

ROSE: Mashing up female monsters.

MARDUKE: Ha ha... Yuh teasin' me, girl. No. No relation as far as I know.

ROSE opens her handbag, takes out notebook and pen, jotting down ideas for song lyrics.

JIMMY: That's it... The Great White God...

MARDUKE: Yuh better check yuh history, boy. De Babylonians was black.

JIMMY: Yuh mean yuh ain' hear about de Great Mutation?

MARDUKE: What yuh talkin' about?

JIMMY: Talkin' about you and me, boy. De Origin of Species in general and white man in particular. When de White God dictator devastate de Garden of Eden wid He all-out nuclear attack, some ah dem black survivor does start ah mutate. Dey skin does bleach and dey dick done shrink. A race of albino Africans limpin' north to conquer de world...

MARDUKE: Is he for real?

ROSE: He's just testing you.

JIMMY: Why not? God is dead, or what? All the Myths are up for grabs.

MARDUKE: White boy losin' he mind, Roy.

ROY: Boy done lost he mind, Marduke sah.

JIMMY: That's how we made 'Voodoo Radio'. Right, Rose? Sampling, man. Sampling is the future.

ROY: I don' know! Ever since Elvis, white man rippin' off we rhythm. Now he come lookin' to steal we God.

JIMMY: I'm not here to rip you off, man. Don't judge us all by Mr Marma-Duke Babylon here. English culture makin' to free up, yuh know. We live in Notting Hill. We've got our own Carnival.

ROY: (*Teasing him.*) It have a white man Carnival?

JIMMY: Well, no, obviously the West Indians started it...

ROY: Trinidadians.

JIMMY: Well, yes, the Trinis, though the Jamaicans seem to be taking over with their heavy sound systems...

ROY: (*Sucks his teeth. Turns to ROSE.*) What yuh doin', Miss? Yuh keepin' a diary?

ROSE: I just got an idea for a new song.

ROY: Yuh want gi' we a sample?

MARDUKE: Now we talkin'!

ROSE: What, now?

ROY: We makin' party, no?

ROSE: I've only just started with it. I haven't got a tune or anything.

ROY: Don' have to be perfect. We samplin', right Jimmy? Come on, girl. Look. I got me drum here.

He brings out a shango drum from behind the reception desk.

We go back yuh up, eh Jimmy?

JIMMY: Yeah. Go on, Rosie, sing something for them.

ROSE: Well... Okay... The first ever performance...

She glances at what she's written, puts the book away.

It's called "Gangster God of Babylon".

ROY: Yuh hear dat, Mistah Marduke? Now dey writin' songs about yuh.

ROSE: Okay. You're the band. The Babylon Boys. Right? You all come in on the chorus: "Ba-Ba-Babylon".

Laughing, the men form a trio: ROY sitting on a barstool with the drum between his legs, MARDUKE behind the desk, JIMMY standing by the other barstool.

Ready? Okay... Gangster God of Babylon, Take One... 2 3 4...

The men beat rhythms on drum, desk and barstool. ROSE, transformed in her performer persona, half-sings, half-speaks the lyric.

I'm the Great Controller
Holy Rock and Roller
I do what I please
Take what I need
All you pretty women get down on your knees
For the Gangster God

MEN: Ba-Ba-Babylon

ROSE: Gangster God of Babylon

The men whoop, drumming her on.

I'm the Great Deceiver
I need a believer
I pump the mass media
Drip, drip-feed ya

Then I come creepin' like a vampire in the night to
    bleed ya
I'm the Gangster God... Kick it!

MEN: Ba-Ba-Babylon

ROSE: Gangster God of Babylon... To the bridge!

Call me MarDuk, you can drop the E
Make sure you never tangle with me
Cos I'm the Great Dictator
Man-ip-ul-a-tor
Yes I'll even con ya
That I'm your Creator
But you find out who ya dealing wid sooner or later
I'm the Gangster God

MEN: Ba-Ba-Babylon

ROSE: Gangster God of Babylon

*The drumming turns to applause, laughter and shouts of
appreciation.*

ROY: Dat were fiery, girl. Yuh makin' all dat up as
yuh go along?

ROSE: I wrote down a few key lines. The first verse... The
rest was improvised... Whatever flashed through my
head...

MARDUKE: I'm not quite sure how I should take that.

ROSE: Why? Was I picking up on something.

MARDUKE: (*Laughs.*) I don' know about that.

ROSE: That's how I write all my songs, just... free
associate...

MARDUKE: (*Laughs heartily.*) Is dat how yuh do it? So
yuh tink I is a bit of a gangster?

ROSE: I'm curious to find out.

MARDUKE: Yuh want see me gun?

He makes a move towards ROSE.

You're very attractive.

ROSE: I know.

MARDUKE: I checkin' yuh out, girl.

ROSE: We're quits then, aren't we?

She turns abruptly away.

What do you think, Jimmy? Calypso? Reggae?

JIMMY: Acid ska! Do a Prince Buster. Police sirens...
Machine-guns... Yeah! And a nuclear bomb to wipe
out the final chorus...

Sings a snatch of the chorus, doing his nuclear bomb effect.

"Gangster God" - whooooomf! Wipe-out!

MARDUKE: Already planning your next big hit?

JIMMY: That's us, man, hit and run. Some of us have to
hustle for our fifteen minutes of fame. You was born
on top, huh? Little Big Boss born and bred...

MARDUKE: I'm sorry to disappoint you, Jimmy, but
you've really no idea of the way things work down
here. My grandparents came over from England after
the First World War, invested in property. The family
fortune made itself, perfectly legally. No shoot-outs in
Woodford Square. No corpses dumped in the harbour.

JIMMY: No skeletons in the cupboard?

MARDUKE: My mother's side goes much further back.
They also intermarried. Me great-great-grandmother
was a pureblood Carib Indian. Dey say she was quite
a beauty too. Yep! Me roots is on me mother's side.

De swamp and jungle done mix wid me blood. I'm what yuh might call a celebrated whitey here in Port of Spain.

JIMMY: So what do they celebrate you for?

MARDUKE: For bein' a winner. All Trinis respect a winner, right Roy?

ROY: Yuh hear, Jimmy? We can still respect a strong white man. But when he weak and crawlin' in de dirt, is hard for black man to have pity.

JIMMY: I can relate to that, as long as your strength isn't based on someone else's weakness. But you know, Mister Marduke, somehow you don't strike me as an out-and-out winner.

MARDUKE: What yuh drivin' at?

JIMMY: What's a rich handsome Winner like you doing all alone in the Hotel Thread in the middle of Carnival?

MARDUKE: (*Laughs, indicating the Soca music blaring in the street.*) I huntin', boy. Yuh hear? "Ah Deputy essential." Watch out, Sheriff, yuh turn yuh back, yuh girl makin' wid de Deputy!

He puts his arm around ROSE, who laughs. He tries to kiss her on the lips. She deftly turns her head away.

Ooops! Sorry. Terribly un-British to be so upfront, isn't it?

ROSE: (*Dryly.*) Not to us.

MARDUKE: You don't mind, do you Jimmy?

JIMMY: I'm not playing the jealous husband just to please you. Rose and I have got a pretty free thing together. You're not the first, Mister Marduke, and you sure as hell won't be the last. If you're really what she's after, I'm not about to slash my wrists. I can have a good time out on my own.

ROSE: Is that where you'd rather be?

JIMMY: Well, sweetheart, do you want him or not?

ROSE: Cut it out, Jimmy. You're both of you making a big deal out of nothing.

ROY: Yuh would let go yuh sweet woman so easy, boy? Dat is a sign yuh 'fraid to get hurt.

ROSE: Look, I just want all of us to have a good time. Okay?

ROY: Right! Let all ah we have a good time and hope nobody get hurt.

MARDUKE: I ain't expectin' nobody to get hurt, Roy.

ROY: I ain't expectin' dat neither.

JIMMY: You're such a tease, Rose. Draw them in and leave them hanging... Just once in a while I'd like to see you perform without the safety net. You know? See you have to finish one of these numbers you pull, follow it through all the way.

ROSE: Jimmy, please! I don't want to fight in public.

JIMMY: What *do* you want, love?

ROY: She want to have a good time! Yuh is deaf or what? Is party all over Port ah Spain tonight, Jimmy. No matter where yuh go, yuh kyan' escape the party.

ROSE: So let's enjoy it while it lasts. Okay?

ROSE starts dancing to the Soca music, now at its loudest in the street. MARDUKE dances with her. JIMMY sits on a bar-stool, helps himself to a drink.

ROY: Yuh was hittin' a bit low just now, boy.

JIMMY: How do you mean, "hittin' low"?

ROY: Yuh ain' hear? How come he all alone tonight... Is
he wife. German girl. Dey say she seein' a black feller
regular yuh know. I tink Mistah Marduke he mean to
kill de man, but I don' know... I tink he 'fraid ah de
man. Yuh see Marduke rich and powerful and do
what he want, but de other feller have another set
power. Is a terrible ting for a man like Marduke. He
won' even talk about it. He have de feelin' everybody
talkin' about him and laughin' behind he back. I tell
yuh, Jimmy, next year dey go write Calypso 'bout
Marduke wife. Now he start drinkin' and when Mistah
Marduke start drinkin' nobody know what go happen.
Yuh better go easy wid he.

*MARDUKE, dancing with ROSE, seems not to hear the
conversation.*

JIMMY: I guess that's the price you pay to play King
Whitey.

ROY: Well now, is not all so black and white, yuh know.
Mistah Marduke is a well-respected man. He know
how to mix wid all kind, and he done help plenty
people wid he money. True it have some say it
leftover from slavery days that one man have so
much land and all.

JIMMY: I wouldn't want it.

ROY: Uneasy sleep de head that wear de crown, eh?
But dem white people pretty smart. Until now yuh
always stay one step ahead ah we.

MARDUKE: (*Stops dancing.*) What yuh say, Roy?

ROY: (*Moving to take ROSE lightly in a formal dancing
pose.*) I say I must show you how to treat a lady,
Mistah Marduke. Yuh no leave she stranded when
she dancin'. True, Miss?

ROSE: (*Playfully imitating him.*) True!

They laugh, dancing cheek to cheek. MARDUKE sits on the bar-stool next to JIMMY, who takes out a spliff.

JIMMY: You got a light?

MARDUKE gives him a light. JIMMY takes a hit, offers it to MARDUKE, who takes a hit, smells it.

MARDUKE: Where do you get this?

JIMMY: Duncan Street...

MARDUKE: Duncan Street! Yuh lucky to get out alive!

JIMMY: Nah! I felt totally safe with them. When I hit town, I always head for the places people tell me not to go. Then I check out the bad boys, the pimps and the dealers, let them know I respect their territory. I make friends with them. Then I score off them.

MARDUKE: (*Chuckles, returning the spliff.*) Den dey rip you off, brother.

He takes out a spliff from his silver cigarette case, offers it to JIMMY.

Try dis. De best Columbian.

He gives JIMMY a light. JIMMY takes a couple of hits, passing it back to MARDUKE, who takes a big hit. They relax.

JIMMY: The Great Integrator. Everyone on this island seems to smoke it, from Laventille shacks to Marduke mansions... Even the police smoke it.

MARDUKE: (*Laughs, coughs, splutters.*) Roy...

He gives ROY the spliff.

I ain' see Commissioner Burroughs smokin' it yet, eh Roy?

JIMMY: (*Passes ROSE his spliff.*) Burroughs... The Kojak man? Shaved head and shades...

ROY: Dat man a star I tell yuh.

JIMMY: Yeah, I seen him on TV the other day.

ROY: Investigatin' de murder?

The spliffs are passed round.

JIMMY: Right. It was amazing. Like they set the whole thing up for the TV. There was a whole bunch of cops standing around staring at the corpse, looking completely disorientated. Then Burroughs shows up, waving a photograph, in full control of the situation. It was like instant animation. Cops crowding in to see the photograph, scurrying off camera like they suddenly know what they've got to do. Cut!

Laughter.

MARDUKE: Yuh got it, boy! A movie.

ROY: Dat man playin' for real I tell yuh! It have some ah dem scamps on de street is only 'fraid ah he.

JIMMY: Did they find the murderer?

ROY: Dey sayin' he a Guyanan. A mariner. Dey say he row out to de Englishman boat in de night. De man choke to death wid a rope around he neck.

ROSE: Was there any motive?

ROY: Money... Though why he have to kill de man I don' know. Is one ah dem blind stroke ah fate.

ROSE: Port of Spain can be a heavy place for whiteys.

ROY: Yuh no 'fraid? No-one go strangle a pretty girl like you.

ROSE: There's plenty of other things they'd do to me given half a chance.

ROY: Is Carnival, no? It have plenty black man want white woman for Deputy. Is a compliment.

ROSE: It doesn't turn me on to be treated like a piece of white meat. You want to know what happened to me tonight? We were dancing in the crowd in Duke Street. I suddenly realised there were only men around us, maybe a hundred men in a tight circle round us, all licking their lips, all hands reaching out to cop a feel... Don't you see, Roy, it's so fucking impersonal!

ROY: Yuh got to make it personal. (*Teasing her.*) When yuh taste de black fruit, den yuh have knowledge.

ROSE: (*Laughing.*) Is that a Biblical come on?

ROY: When yuh taste, den yuh does know.

ROSE: No offence, Roy, but I'm afraid what I might catch if I go round tasting the Carnival fruit.

ROY: Whoo! Now yuh talkin' mean, girl.

ROSE: Well? This is the land of straight-talk, isn't it? The land where you call a fat man Fatman. "Hey Whitey!" "Big Nose!"

ROY: So what yuh callin' me?

ROSE: I'm not calling you anything. It's easy to see that if everyone's fucking everybody else there must be a lot of diseases about.

ROY: I thought that what yuh rock-star doin' all de time. Fuckin' one another... But maybe yuh is really 'fraid to be infected by blackness?

ROSE: Oh! Cut it out, Roy!

ROY: What black and red and go up and down, up and down all night long?

ROSE: I don't know.

ROY: Yuh mudder cunt like a hairy spider!

Only ROY and MARDUKE get the joke.

MARDUKE: Roy, man, I wouldn't tell a joke like that to a lady.

ROY: She don' talk so clean sheself. And I hear dat joke from fourteen year old Carib girl, a sexy fourteen year old wid Carib Indian blood come here to fuck she white boy, tell I she joke.

MARDUKE: You see what sort of a place you've brought her to, Jimmy.

ROY: Is a step up for dem, Mistah Marduke. Dey was stayin' up Laventille.

MARDUKE: In a shack? Is that what yuh mean by a slice of de action?

ROSE: It wasn't what we expected.

MARDUKE: It never is.

He and ROY laugh.

So how de hell yuh end up in a place like dat?

JIMMY: We only arrived last Thursday.

ROSE: We spent our first night in the Bel-Air Hotel...

JIMMY: At the airport...

ROSE: Then Friday morning trudging round hotels and guesthouses. Everything was booked out.

MARDUKE: What yuh expect in de middle of Carnival?

ROSE: Listen, man, I didn't have time to check it out before I came. I work for my money. Huh? This is a ten-day break in one fucking heavy coast-to-coast U.S. tour. That's where I'm coming from, okay?

Awkward silence.

JIMMY: So anyway we're sitting on the grass in Woodford Square and this guy comes over and asks if we need a place to stay.

ROY and MARDUKE burst out laughing in anticipation of a "tourist in the shanty town" story.

ROSE: He was a very sweet guy, and he did his best to make us feel at home.

ROY: He ain' give yuh no trouble?

ROSE: No. He was the perfect gentlemen. I picked up some hot vibes from some of his friends and relations.

MARDUKE: No wonder she's so wired-up, Jimmy. De Hill is no place to take a nice girl like Rose.

JIMMY: There are some good people living up there, man. You should check them out sometime.

MARDUKE: Tomorrow night, Rose, you and Jimmy come and stay with me. Okay?

ROSE: Great! Okay with you, Jimmy?

JIMMY: Sure.

MARDUKE: Sure?

JIMMY: (*Losing patience.*) Look what do you want, man? Me to pat you on the back and tell you you're a good dog or what? Now come on, man! What is it you want from me?

MARDUKE: I don' want or need nuttin' from you, boy.

JIMMY: You're hustling me for something. I can feel it. Is it Rose? Or is it something else you need?

MARDUKE: I'm simply offering you both a place to stay, no strings attached. But maybe you prefer it up in Laventille.

JIMMY: Maybe I do. Maybe I'm not so hooked on your air-conditioned nightmare. "No strings" is funny coming from you, Mister.

ROSE: Jimmy! What's the matter with you?

MARDUKE: A real man of de people, ain' yuh? Well let me tell you, boy, to all ah dem people up Laventille yuh is just a walkin' dollar, and don't you forget it!

JIMMY: Do you walk on your own up Laventille? I doubt it. You got too much to protect, man. Too much to lose.

Imitating MARDUKE.

Dem people up dere can smell it in yuh fadder's money. De blood sweat and tears ah dead slaves. De rottin' corpse ah de Great British Empire!

MARDUKE: Yuh got yuhself a real uptight liberal chip on yuh shoulder dere, boy. Yuh come here five days ago, and now yuh tellin' we how to run we race relations.

JIMMY: De White God Radio Evangelist, blessin' yuh dirty money!

ROSE: Jimmy, shut up! I'm sorry. He gets like this when he's drunk and smoked too much. He likes to provoke...

JIMMY: Come on, Rosie. Wake up! He's no use to you. You can see what he's caught up in. Just another loser whining for a handout.

MARDUKE: Yuh full ah shit, boy!

ROSE: Boys...

ROY: (*In his cheerful storyteller voice, breaking the tension.*) Yuh hear? Man come visit he friend. De man say: "I make a Great Discovery!" He open he bag and pull out a spider. He put it right dere on de table.

Mimes putting the spider on the desk.

Man say: "Spider, run!" Spider run. Man catch it, put it back.

Mimes letting it go, catching it, putting it back.

"Spider, run!" Spider run. "Spider, run!" Spider run.

Repeats mime twice.

Den de man take a razor and he cut off de spider legs. Man say: "Spider, run!" Spider don' run. Man say: "Yuh see? I discover if yuh cut off spider legs, spider kyan' hear yuh no more."

They all laugh, relax.

JIMMY: What's this thing you got with spiders, Roy? Hotel Thread and all... Or is it just coincidence?

ROY: I tink it beginnin' to look like fate, boy. Is timing does bring ting together on dis island. Nuttin' happen by accident. Yuh tink someting it happen. I tink maybe yuh all come here tonight to meet Anancy.

JIMMY: Anancy? We know a band called...

ROY: Anancy de Spider, boy. Come to Trinidad in a slave boat from West Africa. Anancy bring he Shango drum. When he come he find de black man hopeless and dispirited. Anancy start bangin' on he drum. He makin' to play Mas. Anancy de spirit ah music and Mas, de spirit ah Carnival. When dey hit oil in Trinidad, Spider go check it out. He take de oil drum, beat out a Pan. Spider make a steelband, marchin' through de street of Port ah Spain...

ROSE: So that's what all those spiders were doing in the street parade.

MARDUKE: There's a whole body of Anancy folk-tales. He heads this gang of deformed and somewhat disreputable creatures... Drop-leg Goat... Half-face Pig...

ROY: Broken Wing John Crow...

MARDUKE: Anancy's like the Brer Rabbit of the Caribbean...

ROY: Anancy tricksier.

JIMMY: Aha! The Trickster.

ROY: Whoo! Watch out! Yuh tink to sample 'Nancy, boy? He no play yuh way. He make de rule, make dem up as he go 'long. Yuh kyan' ride Spider. He ridin' you!

JIMMY: I hear yuh, 'bro.

ROY: I ever tell yuh, Mistah Marduke, how Anancy de Spider trick Death?

MARDUKE: No, Roy, I don' believe yuh did.

ROY: Remind me to tell yuh dat story sometime.

He turns to ROSE.

Yuh see "African Myth and Legend"?

ROSE: The Mas band? Yes... I think so...

ROY: Dis year I play Spider Mas wid dem.

ROSE: Far out, Roy! Which one were you?

ROY: Yuh probably didn't even notice me. I see you though.

ROSE: Really?

ROY: I see yuh and Jimmy, laughin' about someting in de crowd.

JIMMY: Which were you, Roy?

ROY: Not one ah dem Spider Kings. I no like dem big constructions. I want to be free to move, yuh hear?

ROSE: Will you show us?

ROY: Me Maṣ?

ROSE: Yes, I'd love to see it.

ROY: Yuh want me dress up in me Mas for yuh?

ROSE: Yes. Why not? These guys look like they could use some of that Anancy party spirit.

ROY laughs, disbelieving.

Oh, go on! I bet you look really magnificent. Go on, Roy! For me.

ROY: Yuh real flippy, girl, yuh know dat? If dat what please yuh, I do it.

Turns to leave, stops.

Now yuh people behave yuhselves while I gone, yuh hear? I don' want hear no heavy dialogin'.

MARDUKE: We cool, Roy.

ROY goes out through the interior door. A brief awkward silence.

How yuh feelin', Jimmy?

JIMMY: I don't know what it is, man. I don't know what makes me go for you like that. It's something about this place, the whole situation...

MARDUKE: Yuh don' have to apologise to me. I understand. De Port ah Spain Mas can turn yuh head around. Some ting move into sharp focus, others sink into a big blur. Yuh dig?

JIMMY: Like being inside a film...

MARDUKE: Right. I tell yuh for nuttin', boy, white man stay too long in Trinidad he go ape crazy. Myth and reality get all mix up.

JIMMY: Everybody's private films get cut up together...

MARDUKE: Yuh in yuh own film, boy, and yuh de director. If yuh don' know dat yuh go end up in big trouble. Yuh go find yuhself mix up in all kind ah film.

JIMMY: Your kind of film?

MARDUKE: I ain' say it belong to me, but maybe yuh find yuhself caught up in a Hitchcock thriller, wid me and Roy and dem all involve in a plot to lead yuh to de Hotel Thread where dey have plan to slit yuh throat in de night and sell yuh woman for white slave.

JIMMY: Uh-huh... You getting this, Rose?

MARDUKE: Or maybe a reel creepy horror film wid buckets ah blood and gut and all kind ah black mambo voodoo juju...

ROSE: Peter! Stop it!

MARDUKE: Only teasin'. All right, Jimmy. I tink yuh a bit slow to work out what kind ah film yuh find yuhself in right now, so I go spell it out for yuh. Yuh see Carnival is a sexual vibration. Yuh is out in the middle of it all wid yuh sexy lady, and yuh feeling like she a big bomb all set to explode on yuh. Yuh come in here, hopin' to shut she away from all ah dem hungry black man. But de unexpected happen. Peter Marduke appear on de scene. Yuh see an instant attraction between he and she, a potential Deputy...

ROSE: That's enough. Jimmy's right. These are your movies. You're projecting everything.

MARDUKE: Yuh white cunt all de same. Yuh like a man waiting on yuh every whim. Cockteasers!

ROSE slaps his face. He laughs.

Dat right. I provokin' yuh, girl. I want a reaction. Yuh see, beautiful, it seem to me dat yuh is actin' under Heavy Manners. Yuh know what dat mean?

ROSE: You tell me what it means.

MARDUKE: Put it dis way – is clear enough dat behind dat cool smile yuh Jimmy is a jealous guy.

JIMMY: Jealous! Of you? I wouldn't want to be in your shoes, Mister Marduke. You're sitting on your own bomb and you know it. The Trinidad oil-bomb, the property bomb! Yuh belly full but dem hungry! Yuh know all about dem hungry black man, don't yuh? Yuh is de one trap in a movie, boy. Is yuh is caught up in de crowd ah hungry black man. I ain' see yuh wife tonight. Where is she? Huh? I tell yuh, boy, she out dere somewhere, she fuckin' she black man!

MARDUKE and JIMMY face up to each other, ready to fight. 'Obeah' Soca music in the street, growing louder.

MARDUKE: Yuh is playin' close to de line, white boy. I is on me home ground, don't you forget dat.

JIMMY: But I'm picking up on your history, Marduke. And I'm starting to smell a big rat!

MARDUKE: Yuh cocky little street trash!

JIMMY: Your kind is finished, man! Finished!

MARDUKE hits at JIMMY, who grabs him. They fall to the floor fighting.

ROSE: Jimmy! Peter! Jesus fucking Christ!

The street door opens and MONKEY MAN enters, dancing, leaving the door open. Loud music. He wears combat clothes, a gorilla mask and Che Guevara beret. He holds a paper cup and toy machine-gun in either hand. He moves to ROSE, dancing with her, rolling and thrusting his hips, very sexual, holding the upper part of his body erect. ROSE laughs, relaxed, skilfully evading direct contact. MONKEY MAN drops his cup, spilling red wine. He moves quickly behind ROSE and holds her to him with one hand, covering JIMMY and MARDUKE with the gun.

MARDUKE: (*Calling out uncertainly.*) Roy?

MONKEY MAN ritually fucks ROSE from behind. She laughs crazily. MONKEY MAN moves back towards the street door. JIMMY takes a couple of steps towards him. MONKEY MAN points the gun directly at JIMMY who stops. MARDUKE just stares at ROSE. Exit MONKEY MAN, closing the door behind him. Music fades. ROSE laughs, stops, seeing JIMMY and MARDUKE frozen, staring at her.

ROSE: Hey, zombies! Wake up! Feeding time!

JIMMY and MARDUKE seem to snap out of a trance. JIMMY takes a step towards her.

What is this? Some kind of sleazy sexist racist peep-show? I suppose you'd like to have seen him rape me as well.

JIMMY: Come on, Rose. It wasn't so...

Lights go off. Total darkness. Confusion. ROSE screams.

MARDUKE: What de hell goin' on now? De whole world gone crazy tonight or what?

JIMMY: Rose? Where are you?

ROSE: Jimmy?

MARDUKE: It's me.

ROSE: Don't touch me!

JIMMY: Keep your hands to yourself, mister!

MARDUKE: I didn't...

JIMMY: Who the hell did then?

ROSE: You are dead, man!

JIMMY: Easy, Rosie... Marduke! Where's your fucking lighter?

MARDUKE: Right, boy. Throw some light on de matter.

He lights his lighter, holds the flame up to see ROSE's spooked expression.

Jesus Christ!

The flame goes out. He relights it. ROSE stares like one possessed. She seems to have difficulty breathing.

JIMMY: Rose... What is it?

ROSE: I don't know, Jimmy. I feel so... weird... It's so hot and sticky... I can't breathe! Let me out...

MARDUKE: She really go in for dem big dramatic scene, eh?

JIMMY: Hey, Rosie, this is no time to pull a number... Rose? Rose... Are you okay?

The light of ROY's candles is seen approaching through the interior door.

ROSE: Ah know dis Old Lady... Done swallow de spider...

ROY comes in through the interior, now dressed in his Spider Mas. He wears: a lightweight spiderweb construction strapped around his shoulders and secured on his chest with a yellow clasp, inscribed with a black spider sign; a bulbous rubber head-dress with bubbles suggestive of eyes. Under his Mas he wears only shorts.

He carries a tray of lit candles in one hand, illuminating the scene.

ROY: No panic! Is only a power failure. Happen sometime...

He senses something wrong, moves towards them, holds the tray of candles up to ROSE's face.

Hey! Wha' happenin' here? What goin' on?

MARDUKE: Roy, dat was you? De Monkey Man?

ROY: What nonsense yuh talkin' now?

MARDUKE: It have a man in Mas come in from de street.

ROY: Yuh lookin' scared, boy! All black man does look de same when yuh 'fraid. Wha' happenin', Miss Rose? Yuh lookin' spooked, girl!

ROSE: I done taste de fruit, Roy. Now I does know.

ROY: Hey! Come on now! Jimmy.

He gives JIMMY the tray of candles.

Come on, girl! Snap out! Look at me!

Shakes ROSE, trying to wake her.

What yuh does know?

ROSE: (*Blearily trying to focus on ROY.*) Ah know dis Old Lady done swallow de spider...

ROY slaps her.

JIMMY: Hey!

ROSE: Done stuck in me throat, Roy. Got to spit it out.

ROY: (*Forcing her to look at him.*) Dis another yuh party games, or what?

ROSE: (*Shaking her head loose.*) But ah don' know why Woman swallow de fly...

ROY makes to slap her again.

JIMMY: Roy!

ROSE: (*In a small scared voice.*) Ah tink she die.

JIMMY: Come on, man! You can see for yourself she's way over the top. She's got her head tangled up in some kind of voodoo...

MARDUKE: (*Laughs.*) Now dat what I call a good manager to de last, boy!

ROSE: (*Staring at ROY, whispers.*) Spider... (*Silence.*) Spider...

ROY: What yuh want I do.

ROSE can breathe more easily. She is visibly gathering power in her occult/performer persona. She answers ROY in the voice of a rock and roll shaman.

ROSE: Spider drum, Spider dance
Spider come an' take a chance
Spider want he dance in me body
Spider want yuh drum le' he dance in me body.

ROY: Yuh want I play de big bad black Obeah man for yuh, Miss Rose? Yuh don' know what yuh messin' wid.

ROSE: Ain' have no choice, Roy. Spider done mess wid me.

JIMMY: She's right, Roy. She picked up all this spider shit from you. Least you can do is play along with her, let her work it out of her system. It's her way of dealing when things get too heavy...

ROY: What yuh tink ah dat, Mistah Marduke?

MARDUKE: De boy doin' he best to manage de situation, Roy. But I don' know what to make ah Ramblin' Rose. She want tell de people back home she makin' voodoo wid a real black man? What de hell, Roy. Is Carnival. We in luck, boy. We gettin' a private performance, a live show.

JIMMY: She's too hot for you to handle I tell you, man. You should go home and tuck yourself up in bed.

MARDUKE: Yuh tink yuh white witch go scare me away? Yuh want let she play wid fire is aright by me. But could be your finger get burn.

ROY: Well it seem to me yuh all does have some demon yuh want let loose tonight. Though why yuh have to pick my place I don' know.

He fetches the Shango drum, sits on the bar-stool with the drum between his legs.

Aright. Jimmy... True dat door, in de kitchen, it have salt on de bottom shelf and candle on de table. When Spider dance in Miss Rose body, yuh go throw de salt everywhere. Yuh hear? Dat how we go cut de Obeah.

He gives JIMMY a broad smile and a wink. JIMMY places the tray of candles downstage, takes a candle, and disappears into the darkness behind the interior door.

Aright, Miss Rose. I go drum for yuh, and yuh can dance and shout and jump up and leggo and fall down and roll on de ground and foam at de mouth and anyting else yuh got to do to let it all out. But I ain' messin' wid de dead, yuh hear? We playin' Mas, aright? Mas is to play, lemme tell yuh.

He beats on the Shango drum, exploding in a powerful rhythm. JIMMY returns with salt and candles, moves downstage, attends to candles. ROSE begins to sway to the rhythm, her body shook by sudden spasms. ROY chants.

Obeah Obeah Obeah Obeah Obeah Obeah Obeah
Obeah
I go take yuh sickness I go drive it out
I go take yuh demon I go drum a dem out
Here what I say I de Obeah man
I go drive dem away wid me stick in me hand
Obeah Obeah Obeah Obeah Obeah Obeah Obeah
Obeah

ROSE's movements develop into a simple, repetitive African dance: contracting, releasing. The dance imitates movements of the Spider. Her eyes roll up exposing the whites. She moans, speaks at first with difficulty, but quickly tunes in to the drum rhythm, free-associating, beginning to assume her Spider Queen persona.

ROSE: Spin... Spider... Spinner... Spin the spun thread...
The spun web... Hang from the neck until dead...
Hang from the neck in the Hotel Thread...
Spider crawl... In the mud... Man groves...
Clutching and sucking at my swamp...

ROY's drumming changes rhythm, subsiding to a subliminal background. Eerie steelband music wafts in from the street. JIMMY scatters salt. ROSE moves towards MARDUKE, looking through him.

Come... Come to me... I call you in my sleep. Look!
Here's the hidden path. Here's the way in. See?
Here's the house. Broken windows. Jungle invading
the hallway. Look! A Venus Fly Trap! Don't be
afraid... It's only the spiders. They've had the place
to themselves these last thousand years. Come in...
I'm leading you in. Come... Do you see me now? I'm
dreaming you. I'm dreaming you bending over to
wake me with a kiss...

MARDUKE kisses her. She goes with it for a moment, then reacts as if waking with a start and seeing him for the first time.

MarDuk... You came, at last...

MARDUKE: I ain' come yet, Sleepin' Beauty. Yuh teasin' me all night, girl.

ROSE: Where are my slaves? Jeremiah? Are you sleeping?

JIMMY: No, Miss Rose. I done wake up de same time you do.

ROSE: My swamp perfumes, Jeremiah! My sickly sweet odours! You must smear my body with the black oil of Trinidad. Anoint me, Jeremiah. I am the Spider Queen.

JIMMY moves behind her, mimes smearing her body with oil.

JIMMY: Is true, yuh Highness. Now yuh go marry de Lord MarDuk. De all mighty White God ah Babylon.

ROSE moves away, enters the bedroom which becomes suffused with red light. The hotel lights are still off. She lies down, stretches out on the bed.

MARDUKE: Well I read about yuh European music scene and now I know is all true. It really take a kinky scene to get de bitch on heat, huh? Yuh don' mind, Jeremiah?

JIMMY: Go on, sah. Enjoy yuhself.

As MARDUKE enters the bedroom, ROSE touches her body, the Seductress.

ROSE: Come... Come to me... Come... Into me... I'm every thing that every man in town is hungry for tonight... Hot little bitch... Foxy lady... Come like the spider in my swamp come I swamp you my smell...

As ROSE speaks, MARDUKE takes off his shirt, unbuttons his pants. Seeing his Death Mas, she stops speaking. As he bends down to pull off his pants, she jumps from the bed, startling him.

Is this your sick idea of a joke, MarDuk?

MARDUKE: Is just me Mas. I had it on underneath...

ROSE: Jeremiah! My beasts! Unleash my dragon! My scorpion man! My rabid dog! My spiders! Let bats fly out the moon! MarDuk the Gangster God brings Death into my house...

MARDUKE: Yuh out ah yuh fuckin' mind, girl! I ain' messin' wid yuh!

He pushes his way out of the bedroom, his trousers round his ankles, trips and falls to the floor. ROSE follows him out of the bedroom, crouches over his body like a spider with her prey. The red glow spreads from the bedroom to fill the room. ROY continues drumming. JIMMY snuffs candles, apparently oblivious to ROSE's extraordinary behaviour.

ROSE: True, MarDuk, I a witch... I a voodoo priestess... I de Black Widow spider... I de Spider Queen... I yuh dream come true and deadly...

MARDUKE: (*Struggles to get up, pointing at the wine stain on the floor.*) Wake up, woman! Is blood here on de floor!

ROSE squats astraddle him, pinning him down.

ROSE: Fuck the bitch! Fuck her 'til she bleeds! Trample the witch! Drag her in the dirt! Flay! Stake her to the Earth and let the ant eat her...

MARDUKE: Jimmy! Dat Monkey Man cup full ah blood!

JIMMY: (*Imitates the voice of the American Evangelist heard earlier on the radio.*) Is true Father MarDuk, and praise the Power in the Blood we're all still here. I'm Brother James, on hand to help and advise. You know Moses had this same problem all those years ago. And what Moses did when he got to Heaven, he walked right up to those Immigration Officers and he said: "I want to talk to your Superior. I want to talk to the Boss!" Well those Immigration Officers they thought he was pretty weird, but he was so persistent they finally let him through and they took him up to Head Office...

ROSE: Wake her up in a peepshow cabin...
Put her in her place, come on her face and...
Watch her reflect your own projection...
Watch her Watch her Watch her Watch her Watch her–Watch out!

JIMMY: God took one look at Moses, and He spoke like he was reading Moses' mind. He said: "Moses, ya know that lamb ya slaughtered? The Blood of the Lamb is your protection. There is Power in the Blood! Roast it, Moses! Roast that lamb!"

ROSE: (*Ritually fucking MARDUKE.*) Tie bitch! Fuck stake! Flog! Flay! Bleed!

She convulses in an agonizing climax, collapses on top of MARDUKE.

JIMMY: That's right! The Blood of the Lamb is your free passport to paradise. And here at the White God Radio Mission we don't just fatten the lamb, we slaughter and roast it as well...

MARDUKE: (*Throws off ROSE, scrambles to his feet, hitches up his pants, shouting.*) Shut up!

For the first time since ROY began drumming, there is silence in the room. A cold blue-white light.

Yuh crazy! All ah yuh! All dat musical madness done mash up yuh brains!

Holding up his pants with one hand, he pushes past JIMMY to the desk.

Get out ah de way! I need a fuckin' drink!

He pours himself a stiff drink, drinks.

ROY: Dem not so crazy, boy. Dey lettin' it all out, all de frustration and madness, lettin' it all out in one big party. I t'ought dat what yuh wanted.

MARDUKE: (*Delirious.*) What yuh done wid me wife, Roy? Where yuh hidin' she? Huh? Yuh got she hidden away in de back room?

ROY: Yuh is tight as a kite, boy... Wha' happenin', Mistah Marduke? Yuh come here tonight to spook me out wid yuh Death Mas, yuh put a hex on dis young woman who never done yuh no harm, yuh set de scene for a big showdown wid de white boy here, and now yuh 'fraid?

MARDUKE: Dem makin' monkey out ah you and me, Roy. Yuh little singer witch, she bring she own bad trip along wid she. Now she feel yuh protectin' she, she feel safe to fuck around wid me.

ROY: Well now I don' pretend to understand all de level, but it seem to me, Mistah Marduke, dat dis woman have issue some strong allegation against you, and I tink, sah, dat you would be wise to answer she.

MARDUKE: Yuh is a fool, Roy!

ROY: Please answer de question, sah.

JIMMY: (*Drunkenly goading MARDUKE.*) Right! Act out yuh part, sah! Le' we see Death de handsome millionaire, de cold mean white master. Wha' happenin', sah? Yuh is in yuh own movie, or wha'?

MARDUKE: Yuh don' know what yuh dealin' wid here, boy. Yuh is just playin' chicken on de railway line, yuh hear!

He takes a last long drink, puts down his glass with an air of finality.

Aright, Jimmy... Russian roulette. We already got de blood on de carpet.

He pulls off his pants, becomes physically more powerful in his Death Mas.

Aright, Roy... Yuh ready for de Gangster God?

ROY: Stop beatin' round de bush, boy. Gi' it to we straight.

MARDUKE: Gangster God ah Babylon. Take Two... Three, Four...

ROY drums. JIMMY beats on the desk. ROSE laughs. MARDUKE chants.

I de Mighty Persuader
De Space Invader
To all de sick people
I look like a Saviour
Darkness at noon, zombies risin' from de grave
For de Gangster God...

ROY *and* JIMMY: Ba - Ba - Babylon

MARDUKE: De Gangster God ah Babylon.

He picks up his doctor's bag, puts it on the desk, opens it. To JIMMY, rapping over the rhythm.

True, boy, de Gangster God ah Babylon. I runnin' dis fuckin' freakshow! I got all ah dem lives in de palm ah me hand. I decides if dem live...

He reaches into the doctor's bag.

Or die.

He pulls out a gun, points it at ROY, who stops drumming.
JIMMY and ROSE start at the sight of the gun.

ROY: (*Shows no trace of fear.*) Yuh don' shoot dat ting ah me, Marduke.

MARDUKE: (*Holds his aim for several seconds, then, laughing, lets his arm fall.*) True, Roy. I don' kill Roy. I only askin' yuh one favour. Yuh let me play Mas one last time...

ROY: Yuh know me, boy. I ain' forbid nuttin' in Carnival. Play Mas, Marduke. Don' take it all so personal.

MARDUKE: (*Moves to ROSE.*) Aright... Yuh see dis gun, Miss? I go give yuh dis gun for safe keepin'. I tink I can trust yuh. I see yuh come out ah yuh trance...

ROSE: I don't want it...

MARDUKE: (*Points the gun at her.*) Yuh don' take it, I go use it, woman!

JIMMY: Marduke!

MARDUKE puts the gun into ROSE's hand. She has not predicted this turn of events and is evidently out of her depth.

MARDUKE: One last game, Jeremiah?

JIMMY: Fly on yuh shirt, sah.

He brushes something from MARDUKE's shirt.

MARDUKE: Yuh learnin' fast, boy. I educatin' yuh, right?

JIMMY: True, sah! Ah educated nigger is next best ting it have to white skin.

MARDUKE: Right, boy! We come to raise dem up from de swamp!

He reaches into the doctor's bag, takes out his Mas gloves, puts them on, becomes aware of ROSE staring at him.

What yuh starin' at, witch? Is true I Death, girl. De Earth shake where I walk. De dogs howl. Death walk de Carnival street tonight.

JIMMY: Sah! Dem hungry black man is at de door again! Dem shoutin' to come in, sah! What I should tell dem, sah?

MARDUKE: Tell dem Death preparin' heself for dem. Tell dem Death waitin' to meet all ah dem.

He takes out the Death mask, walks slowly towards ROSE, holding up the mask as a second face.

Is true I Death, girl. I de wild card in de Carnival. Nobody know where I go shoot next. Now in dis gun yuh holdin' it have six chamber. Two ah de chamber have bullet. De odds is two to one each way. Yuh hear? Yuh Obeah man done steal me power when he fuck me wife. Yuh finish me off, girl. Now yuh go point dat ting at me and pull de trigger...

ROSE: You're crazy...

MARDUKE puts the Death mask over his head.

Jimmy, do something. This is past a joke.

JIMMY: True, Rose. We all waitin' for de punchline.

ROSE: Roy...

ROY: Yuh spin web, yuh catch fly. Ain' nuttin' to do wid me, Miss. If dat what de man want, I ain' go stop him.

JIMMY: Is de kindest ting to do, Rose, like puttin' a poor sick wounded dog out of its misery... Yuh hat, sah.

MARDUKE takes his top hat from JIMMY, puts it on. He is now dressed as when he first appeared.

ROY: I ain' even here. I ain' here at all. I out in de street de whole night playin' Mas wid me friends. I got witness. Plenty people seen me...

JIMMY: Roy return. He find de corpse all dress up as Death...

ROSE: Jimmy! What the fuck are you playing at?

JIMMY: Commissioner Burroughs come hurryin' to de scene ah de crime. But Rose and Jimmy vanish in de night. No witness. De classic Carnival murder mystery.

ROY: Yuh see wha' happen when white people go messin' wid Anancy.

MARDUKE advances slowly towards ROSE, his arms outstretched to embrace her.

ROSE: This isn't a game any more. This gun's real.

JIMMY: He's bluffing, Rose. The gun's empty.

ROSE: You're insane! All of you! You're trying to turn me into... Marduke!

MARDUKE has her cornered. She points the gun at the ceiling, firing one shot in the air. MARDUKE staggers backwards, clutching his chest, collapsing in the rocking-chair. ROSE and JIMMY stare at him in stunned silence. ROY moves towards him, holding the newspaper, speaking in his storyteller's voice, as SPIDER, to audience.

SPIDER: Anancy come to de House ah Death. Anancy askin' Mistah Death: "How come it have no people here?"

MARDUKE (as DEATH) makes a large shrugging gesture. Soca music in the street, far away.

Mistah Death he say: "Some ah dem come, but dem no stay long." Anancy stay de night in de house ah

Death, but he don' sleep. He know Death only take yuh when yuh sleepin'... Bzzz... Fly on yuh shirt, sah! Is bad luck. Here!

SPIDER swats the fly with his folded newspaper.

Here, sah!

SPIDER gives DEATH the newspaper.

Anancy de Spider run out into de garden and away. Mistah Death he get so vex, he chasin' Spider all de way. But now he come to de place where all de ant is come to meet Anancy. Now yuh all must know, Mistah Death he like nuttin' better than to eat de ant. Now he see before him de feast of a lifetime. He hollow eye open wide. He pickin' dem up wid he bony finger.

DEATH swats himself with the newspaper.

He bendin' down like he make to lick all ah dem up, but yuh know Mistah Death... He no Tongue Man...

MARDUKE passes out: DEATH falls limp in the rocking-chair.

Anancy he say: "River, flood!" River flood. "River, burst yuh banks, yuh go flood all de Earth, yuh go wash it all clean!" De river doin' as Spider say, and Mistah Death he kyan' cross de water. Spider leave he stranded on de other side...

SPIDER sets the chair rocking.

Spider he return to dem mad monkey street...
he spinnin' an' swirlin'...
he jump up and leggo...
he limin' he winin'...
he dancin' he dancin'...
he dancin' he dancin'...

Soca music hits fever-pitch as SPIDER dances out through the street-door, leaving MARDUKE slumped in the rocking chair. ROSE and JIMMY stare at him without moving.

Blackout.

The End

DEAD MAN'S HANDLE

CHARACTERS

The MAN

The WOMAN

The DOCTOR

DEATH

Dead Man's Handle was first performed by Soho Theatre Company and directed by Alex Perrin.

The set is minimal: an orthopaedic bed; tubes and wires linking the body to a life-support machine; a chair.

A hospital intensive care unit

The MAN is in a coma, propped-up in bed, his inert body connected to a ventilator, various drips, ECG and other sensors wired to a life-support machine: a faint steady bleep monitors his heartbeat. His medical report hangs on the bed, with a scrawled note: "Nil by mouth".

The WOMAN stands staring at him, in shock. She has a folded newspaper under her arm.

The DOCTOR brings her a glass of water. She takes it from him without reacting.

DOCTOR: It's okay... I don't mean... I mean I... I don't think... I don't think what you're going through is ever easy... for anyone. I have to say, I do think you're coping remarkably well.

The WOMAN shakes her head.

But – oh, I think you are! But I think – I mean I don't think anyone can go through what you're going through and hold it all... you know... you've got to – got to – cry for him and... give yourself time to think it through – start to – come to terms... and I think it's good that – that's what you're starting to do. I do think... if we're going to – talk it through... I er... I think you'd better sit down.

He offers her the bedside chair. The WOMAN seems not to notice, staring at the MAN in bed. The DOCTOR coughs.

As I said, we're going to have to look at the scans in more detail. But – I'm afraid it does – does look as if there is very severe and extensive damage to his brain. Now, what this means... we can keep him alive, in a stable condition but... the fact is... that to all intents and purposes – the only things keeping his heart beating and – that sort of thing... are the drugs and the – the fact that he's on the ventilator.

The WOMAN stares blankly at the DOCTOR.

DOCTOR: The thing is... as things stand... the most we can do is – is to maintain him in some sort of – half-life. In this sense we – as doctors – we can't heal him... we're reduced to – we're really no more than... technicians...

The WOMAN sips her water.

I know it's hard – when you care for someone – even if they don't even know you exist... it's – as if you – you somehow invest them with life. But – as I said – it does – does look as though the damage is irreversible. Okay?

WOMAN: (*Pulling herself together.*) Thank you, Doctor. Would you mind if I sat with him for a while?

DOCTOR: Not at all. You may wish to talk to him. Perhaps he can hear you. Who knows? There is still *some* evidence of brain-activity. Who knows what's going on in there. Of course, you do hear of cases – patient in a coma responding to a familiar voice... but in his case – frankly...

WOMAN: Can I hold his hand?

DOCTOR: I don't see why not, but do mind the drip. I do think... we do have to – face the fact – he isn't going to get any better. Sooner or later I think we're going to have to – you know – to... think through some very hard... things... I think. Okay?

The WOMAN nods. Exit DOCTOR.

WOMAN: (*To MAN.*) Well, that was the *good* news!

She laughs nervously. She stares at the water in the glass, looks for a table, finally puts it on top of the life-support machine. She sits on the chair by the bed, speaking as if he can hear her, adopting a breezy, innocuous tone.

Sorry I'm late. Took me forever to get here. Incident on the Piccadilly Line... You won't believe this – they had a runaway tube train! Driver gets out to check the door. Train pulls out, rattles on through the next station. So then of course, the whole system grinds to a halt while they check the line. We were stuck in the tunnel for over an hour. By the time we got out it was in the late edition.

She opens her evening paper, scanning the report, as if keeping him up to date with the news.

Apparently it's technically possible for trains to move without the driver – although the brakes are supposed to engage automatically if the driver's handle – it's funny, they call it the "dead man's handle"... is... released...

Her voice trails off. She throws down the paper, gets up and lights a cigarette, pacing around the bed, distractedly taking several drags before she realises she's smoking in a hospital.

Oh, God – what am I doing?

She stamps out the cigarette.

Be just like me to go and set off the alarms.

She sits back down, staring at the MAN. Pause.

Hello... It's me. Remember? Are you there? Hello? Anyone there? You always think somehow there'll be... time... to say the things you... And then it's too late... No-one to hear it...

Pause.

Listen! I don't want to lose you. But, to see you like this... reduced to... I know. It's selfish... I say to myself "For *your* sake. I don't want you to suffer" – but what I mean is "*I* don't want to *see* you suffer." I just... can't bear this... dead weight of seeing someone I love slowly wasting away before my eyes. I want to close my eyes and picture you as I knew you, with all your faculties intact. But this... This isn't you. Is it? If they could heal you, somehow... restore you, make you whole again... But if they can't, I wish... I wish they'd just let you...

Pause. She takes his hand.

I had a dream about you... We were in Mexico. It was the Day of the Dead – dancing skeletons and ragged-arsed street-kids with trays full of sugar skulls and... I lost you in the crowd. I couldn't find you... One of the urchins handed me a note in your handwriting. It said you wanted a divorce... And I thought to myself – but we're not even married...

Pause. She strokes his hand.

You remember Mexico? Some honeymoon, huh? Remember that horrendous night-bus to San Cristobal?

She is lulled into a trance-like passivity.

In the dream, I kept staring at your note, and suddenly I could see... It was a fake. Someone had forged your handwriting. And I knew that something terrible had happened to you...

The MAN's head moves. He mumbles incoherently. She bends closer to hear.

Yes? What was that?

MAN: El Dia de los Muertos...

WOMAN: The Day of the Dead. Yes... In my dream...

MAN: Shoeshine boy...

WOMAN: Yes, there were shoeshine boys... But I couldn't find you anywhere...

The MAN sits slowly up. His eyes open, but seem to look through her.

MAN: "Shine, Mister? This way, senor. Follow me." Cross-fade to mountain village...

WOMAN: I don't understand... This was **my** dream...

MAN: I know. I was there. I wanted to wait for you, but I had to follow the shoeshine boy... The old men show me a codex printed on cheesecloth... glyphs and... cyphers... moving pictures... Trick is to see through them, through to the Other Side... over there – on the other side of the world – everything we think or dream – the Old Gods are alive... Government troops ransack the mountain village – lay waste the mysteries – but they're too late – the Old Gods have crossed over – over to the Other Side – they'll never find them, never... But they found me...

WOMAN: H-How...

MAN: I escaped... But they found me. They caught me. They brought me back...

He looks about him, confused.

It's snowing...

WOMAN: Not now... We had snow last week. In London...

MAN: Snowing...

WOMAN: Do you know where you are?

MAN: White room... electrical hum... bleep bleep bleep... that's the Ghost. Ghost in the Machine.

Don Juan says you have to wrestle with Death like a warrior. But it's hard, when you're being held in "some kind of half-life", incubated by "body technicians"... held hostage by the medical mafia... (*Becoming more animated.*) Now the Tibetans – they wrote the guide-book, Life After Death, where to catch the bus to the next Bardo – they don't fuck with the corpse. Chop chop. Feed it to the crows. Crow black... red meat... snow white... bone...

He is holding forth, delirious.

Cross-fade to Bali... Cremation towers – riot of feathers and flowers... Come to the crossroads and it's – Spin, boys! Confuse-A-Ghost – spin us round and round, bang your gongs till we lose our bearings – speed us on our way so's we don't come back to haunt you! Talk about a send-off! The towers are rockets! And the cremation ground? It's a launch-pad! They're launching their dead into eternity.

He gesticulates excitedly.

WOMAN: Mind the drip.

MAN: Fuck the drip!

He draws her closer, lowering his voice.

You see? White magic...

The WOMAN shivers. The MAN is raving.

MAN: Our witch doctors practice the Black Arts. They found a way to trap the ghost in the – the machine. Immortality in the flesh... but... addiction to a body deforms the spirit – all of us, stifled, shut down by the fear of death... Once they've killed the spirit, they're free to carve up the flesh any way they want – hook up our brains – tape our dreams – determine the existence or otherwise of the Hereafter... Case of M. Valdimar... death by putrefaction...

WOMAN: Stop it! Please. Why? Why?

MAN: To help you...

WOMAN: Help *me*?

MAN: To do...

WOMAN: What?

MAN: What you came here to do.

WOMAN: To be honest, I don't know why I came –
what I was hoping to... Do you know who I am?

MAN: Yes. And now you're here...

WOMAN: Finally... (*Awkwardly.*) I had a dream...

MAN: I know. I was in it. I know why you came...

WOMAN: No! I don't want to know.

MAN: You came to release me.

WOMAN: No!

MAN: Set me free.

WOMAN: No! This isn't happening. Oh, God!

The WOMAN buries her face in her hands, crying.
The MAN touches her, comforting.

MAN: Hey! Hey! It's okay! I'm here. Hey! Don't leave
me here. I need you...

WOMAN: This can't be you. This is my own mind
talking to me. My own lousy guilt...

MAN: What have you got to be guilty about? You
want my forgiveness? There's nothing to forgive...
Forget the bad fucks. Thank God for the good ones.

WOMAN: Come on! There was more to us than
fucking.

MAN: Hey! I'm a man, okay. My brain's fucked. At least I can think with my dick.

WOMAN: There's nothing wrong with your brain.

MAN: Then how come I'm talking to you now? I may be brain-damaged, but I'm not brain-dead. I'm painfully aware of my own predicament. Severe and extensive damage to the left hemisphere – that explains the visions and the voices... But the real damage is here – in the brain-stem – my reticular activating system – it isn't – firing or switching or whatever – the messages – from my brain to my body... I'm not getting through. I can't wake up! To all intents and purposes I've been dead for months.

Reacting to an invisible adversary.

What? What's that? Frankly? Frankly what, doc? Frankly, doc, I'm fucked. Now fuck off!

Turning to the WOMAN with a paranoid grin.

Sorry about that. Auditory hallucination. See? I can't be talking to you. How could I? You're not even here. All in the mind. It was all I had left, my brain, and now that's fucked... I'm totally... terminally... fatally... fucked...

MAN looks about him, disorientated, then sinks back on the bed, relapsing into his coma. WOMAN clutches him, shaking him.

WOMAN: No... I *am* here. I hear you. I'm not just a figment of your imagination. Can you hear me? Please! This is important. Where are you?

MAN: (*Mumbling in his delirium.*) Machine...

WOMAN: Yes... The witch doctor trapped your ghost in his machine. And now I'm going to set you free. I'm going to disconnect you... Okay?

She begins disconnecting the drips and sensors from the MAN's body: the bleep stops. The MAN revives, stares at her in shock.

Well? Are you just going to lie there and wait for death to come and take you? You do that, you're as good as dead already! Wake up! Time to get up – get your act together. Come on, darling! What would Don Juan say? You want to trick death? You hunt him like a warrior, stalk him, take him by surprise... *YOU* take *HIM.*

MAN: But... I... I can't move...

WOMAN: You can. You must. Try!

With an enormous effort, the MAN slowly rises from his bed. She takes his hand, helping him, before letting him walk unaided. He moves clumsily, like a somnambulist, then stops, staring at the WOMAN, as if seeing her for the first time.

MAN: I know you.

WOMAN: Who am I?

MAN: The Bruja...

WOMAN: Brew-ha?

MAN: A witch, but... Not evil... No... White witch... Yes... Bruja!

WOMAN: Brew-ha? As in...

BOTH: Brouhaha!

They laugh.

MAN: Why are you here?

WOMAN: To cure you.

She fetches the half-full glass of water.

Here. Witches brew.

She hands him the glass of water.

MAN: What's in it?

WOMAN: The usual... Eye of newt... Wing of bat... Dash of menstrual blood...

MAN: To appease the Gods?

WOMAN: No, the blood is to impress the men. It's not easy being a witch in a world like this. Drink!

The MAN drinks the water. His eyes are open but seem to be looking through the world, into another. He approaches the bed, examining the trailing drips and sensors.

WOMAN: Where are you?

MAN: Tendril... creeper... jungle...

WOMAN: Sounds like we're back in Mexico.

MAN: White room... the body on the bed... machine going bleep bleep bleep...

WOMAN: That's the trap... the ghost-trap...

MAN: Double exposure... But I see through it, right through to the – Other Side – and it's right here, worlds within worlds, encoded, inside the white room... I decode jungle...

WOMAN: Enter jungle... Leave the white room...

MAN: I enter... I cross over...

WOMAN: You escaped once... You can do it again...

MAN: Going out... Crossing over... Over and out...

WOMAN: No, not yet, don't lose contact. Tell me where you are. Describe it to me.

MAN: I'm on a cliff, looking out over the Gulf... Ships sail into the bay, Spanish galleons... Conquistadors... come to lay waste the Old Gods, plunder the mysteries... Cut to bird's-eye view... black crow, looking down from an empty blue... sky... And I laugh – caw-caw-caw – they cannot conquer what they cannot see...

He comes out of his trance, blinking. They embrace. He is shivering.

WOMAN: Oh, you're burning! You're supposed to be cold! Is this what they mean by life after death?

MAN: No proof either way. We could be dealing with a near-death experience, or the moment of death infinitely extended... Who knows? Maybe us ghosts just burn up without our wetsuits. In which case, I don't have much time... I'm going after him... I have to go... go on... alone... And you... have to stay... Live... and let... go... Tell them... death drives the engine... but... love... blows... the whistle...

He kisses her, then walks purposefully away, sinking back into his trance, rocking to the movement of an invisible tube-train.

WOMAN: What? What kind of goodbye is that. "Love blows the..." What the fuck is that supposed to mean? Wait! Where? Where are you going? Where are you?

MAN: London Underground...

WOMAN: The Tube?

MAN: Piccadilly Line... The carriages jolting and clashing and the lights keep flashing off, on off on, off...

WOMAN: Am I in the carriage?

MAN: No... No, this time I'm alone... walk down the
empty carriage... through the connecting door
and... into the next carriage... Empty... Train jolts,
lurches. Lights flashing off, on off on, off... Walk
down... through the second door and... into the
third carriage... Not a soul... And it dawns on me,
down here in the dark, there's no driver... It's the
Runaway Train, rattling through disused tunnels...
Dead Man's Handle... This is a Ghost Train, and
I'm the ghost... alone with... my Death... waiting for
me behind that third door... But this time, I'm ready
for him... This time I'm not afraid... I'm walking
down the carriage... I open the third door...

*As he "opens" the door, DEATH appears, in surgical
cap and gown with a grinning skull-mask, facing him
in a mirror-image.*

And here he comes, right on cue, like a Mex
cartoon on the Day of the Dead... Doctor Death,
Skull and Sawbones... Not afraid of you...This
time... I know what to do... raise you... two fingers
and... bang!

*He "shoots" DEATH, who crumples, "dies". The MAN
calmly gets back in bed.*

What's up, Doc? Your whole world of fear... death
and decay... just... blow them away. End of the
line, folks! End of the tunnel. And... there's Light.
There's space and light and... black crow...
flapping... in the... empty... blue...

The MAN dies.

*The WOMAN, frozen in a stark white light, alone, at
breaking point.*

Blackout.

The End

ICEMAN

It was the sole commandment that ran there:

"Thou shalt not nark."

Arthur Morrison *Child Jago* 1896

CHARACTERS

BUZZ, a man in his twenties.

ALICE, a woman in her thirties.

CROWE, a man in his forties.

ACT ONE

A basement in an old warehouse. The brick vault has been partially transformed into the "Quetzal Travel" agency, a bucket-shop offering discount plane-tickets.

Upstage right: a barred security gate leading to a passage.

The office is sparsely furnished with a couch (right) and a desk (left) with telephone, intercom etc; swivel chairs on either side. A reproduction of the Aztec calendar and a sign bearing the legend QUETZAL TRAVEL, hang on the wall behind the desk.

Along the back wall there is a display-rack with travel brochures and a unit housing a TV and an abstract "bird" made of fragments of mirror-glass. The bird conceals a video camera connected to the TV.

Upstage left: a coffee machine stands on top of the solitary filing cabinet.

Downstage left: a section of the brick wall opens, like a secret door, onto an empty stairwell.

The place has a transient feel, with certain incongruities and estranging features: the bars of the security gate suggest a cell-door. It may look more like a studio set than the real thing.

Darkness. The TV screen lights up. A shifting mosaic of flesh-tones resolves itself into a computer-processed FACE, the voice similarly treated to disguise the speaker's identity. The video clip shows the debriefing of a police informer or undercover agent. An off-screen voice (CONTROL) asks the questions.

CONTROL: Ice Man?

FACE: Ice, Snow, Rain – you name it – the Man can deliver – bulk!

Lights up on BUZZ, wearing a sharp suit and tie, sat at the desk smoking a spliff, watching the video.

CONTROL: You say he's one of ours. (*Pause.*) Can you be more explicit?

FACE: Hard to put your finger on. (*Pause.*) Patterns... Dealer gets busted; Iceman moves in to take his place. (*Pause.*) The coke dries up; we all start smoking crack.

The phone rings. BUZZ takes another hit, presses a hidden button: TV screen goes blank. BUZZ answers the phone.

BUZZ: Quetzal Travel... She's not here right now... This is her secretary. Can I take a message? Crow... Uh-huh? The block booking. Uh... Can she call you back, Mr Crow? She won't be long. Just popped out for some uh...

The door-bell rings.

Hang on...

TV screen shows ALICE, in the street, seen through a security camera. BUZZ pushes another button.

BUZZ: Mr Crow? Can you hold? She's on her way down.

ALICE appears outside the barred cell-door, wearing a coat and clutching a bag of coffee. BUZZ takes a bunch of keys, unlocks the door, gesturing at the phone.

Early bird...

ALICE glances at her watch, frowning. She goes to the desk, picks up the phone.

ALICE: Hello? Hi, Crowe. You're early. Hmm? Oh, yeah... He was minding the store. No. No, he's on his way out. (*Signals to BUZZ, calling out for effect.*) Thanks. Bye!

BUZZ noisily slams the cell-door shut. ALICE listens on the phone, reacting.

What, now? Er... Well... Okay. Gimme ten. Okay? Okay.

Puts down the phone, decisively.

Okay, Buzz, we got ten minutes.

Sniffs the air.

BUZZ: No sweat, babes. We all set.

ALICE: You run the rig?

BUZZ: Rig sharp, man! Razor! Need something for the levels.

BUZZ opens the secret door in the wall, disappearing through it. ALICE takes off her coat. She is dressed in an attractive business suit. She rummages in the filing cabinet for air-freshener, sprays the room. Puts coffee in the filter, switches on the machine. She moves around the room, casually striking poses for the hidden camera, doing her sound check.

ALICE: Testing. Testing... One two, one two... "Iceman"... Take one... One... One two...

Paces nervously. The coffee machine hisses, dripping hot coffee into the jug. BUZZ returns through the door in the wall.

BUZZ: Hey, babes, you seen my – (*Stops short, admiring her outfit.*) Nice!

ALICE: Have I seen your what?

BUZZ: (*Blank.*) What?

ALICE: How am I supposed to know? Hello? Anyone home? Are we receiving?

BUZZ: Loud and clear! (*Appraises her.*) You really go to town on this one.

ALICE: (*Shrugs.*) Our best customer.

BUZZ: Big time, babes. You're not careful, you start showing up on computers and shit. Here's your sample. (*Hands her a ziplock bag of Ice crystals.*) He might want to cook up a freeze.

ALICE: (*Examines the sample.*) How much do I give him?

BUZZ: As much as he can take. The harder they come...

ALICE: You're an evil fuck.

BUZZ: Been there, babes. Paid my dues.

> *BUZZ opens the filing cabinet and takes out a bottle and dropper, showing her.*

The Truth. Doctor B's special remedy.

> *BUZZ measures a few drops from the bottle into a coffee cup, then, as if offering it to a guest.*

BUZZ: "Coffee?" (*Hands her the cup.*) Take about an hour to come on. Try to get some down him before he samples. And whatever you do, don't mix your cups, or you're in for a big surprise, girl!

ALICE: (*Sniffs the cup, suspiciously.*) You sure this stuff is safe?

BUZZ: The Truth always involve an element of risk. (*Laughs.*) Safe, man! I'm your living proof, the original detox-man. I proved it can be done. (*Playing the director.*) Cue music!

> *Music blasts out. He raps over it.*

Welcome to the Killing Floor
Don't ask me what we fightin' for
Welcome to the Twilight Zone...

ALICE: Okay. Cut. Cut! (*Music stops abruptly.*) I hope there's someone up there checking the levels.

BUZZ: It's all under control.

Watches her, sensing her unease.

Just remember, babes. Nothing personal...

ALICE: What the fuck is that supposed to mean?

BUZZ: You get what you need. You get the fuck out!

ALICE: What's your problem, Buzz?

BUZZ: Oh, no problem, babes. It's your number. I'm
well out of it.

ALICE: I can see that! (*Defensively.*) He's a john, okay?
Another fucking john!

BUZZ: Good.

Pause. They eye one another.

ALICE: Fuck you!

BUZZ: Anytime, babes. Anytime. (*Surveys the room.
Struck by a thought.*) Oh, Sylvia, before I forget –

ALICE: Alice. It's Alice. Christ, Buzz, I've been Alice
for the last month.

BUZZ: I think I prefer Sylvia.

ALICE: Try, Buzz. It does tend to give the game away.
(*Irritably.*) Well? What?

BUZZ: What?

ALICE: What you have to tell me before you forget.

BUZZ: Oh, yeah! (*Thinks, draws a blank.*) Too late!

ALICE: You fucking spacehead! What we on today, huh?

BUZZ: Chill out, babes. Only smoke an 'ickle spliff.

ALICE: How many times, man – when we're on a job, I
need you straight!

BUZZ: You been known to have an 'ickle puff. Anyhow, wasn't me forgot to buy coffee and had to –

ALICE: Okay, Buzz, just try to keep it together, okay? When I'm done with him I'll pass him on to you. Until then, you sit tight, upstairs.

BUZZ: At the controls.

ALICE: Not a peep.

BUZZ: I'm not even here.

ALICE: And then?

BUZZ: You call the Man. I log the call. Out the back... Go catch a pizza...(*Frowns, reconsidering their plan of action.*) I could send out for a take-away. Have a bite upstairs, where I can keep an eye on you.

ALICE: (*Patient but firm.*) Buzz...

BUZZ: I don't like leaving you alone with the Crow.

ALICE: Buzz... If you don't go out, how the fuck do you come in? Hmm? You come in the front – hopefully looking like you've come from someplace else.

BUZZ: Yeah, but... (*Frowns.*) I'm the source, right?

ALICE: No! Come on, man. Focus! The source can't come here. That's the whole point. The whole fucking point is the source remains hidden.

BUZZ: Oh, yeah, right! So, who am I, then?

ALICE: His bagman.

BUZZ: (*Winding her up.*) Whose bagman?

ALICE: The source! The Iceman!

BUZZ: Oh! I see.

ALICE: The Iceman doesn't come in person.

BUZZ: (*Grins.*) How could he?´

ALICE: Exactly.

BUZZ: Oh! So I'm with him. I get it.

ALICE: You're nothing to do with me.

BUZZ: I never clapped eyes on you.

ALICE: Good. (*Pause.*)

BUZZ: But... What if I have to come down?

ALICE: You don't come down. That's what we've just established beyond any shadow of a doubt. You don't come down. You stay up.

BUZZ: It's your number, babes, but I can see a situation where I may *have* to come down.

ALICE: What the fuck is this?

BUZZ: What do you know about the john? John Crow. You don't even know he's the man you're after. What if he's the man after you? Has to be one. That's how it works... Man places an order this size you think twice. Then you think a whole lot more. Who's behind him? Who gives his orders?

ALICE: Who says he's acting under orders?

BUZZ: Who says he isn't? What if it's *his* set-up, with you stuck in the frame. Stitch you up like that!

ALICE: If he tries anything, I don't need you busting in with your Rambo routine.

BUZZ: He'll have back-up.

ALICE: If he has, it's been taken care of.

BUZZ: Assuming your orders can stiff the Crow's.

ALICE: I have to act on that assumption. (*Pause.*)

BUZZ: And if the Face fit, you got some strung-out speed-freak with a gun and a headful of Ice –

ALICE: Thanks, Buzz. I'll call if I need you.

BUZZ: I'll be listening.

ALICE: You just make sure you get it all down. (*Tense pause.*) So... We were saying...

BUZZ: Shit! (*Grins, rolling up his sleeve to reveal a remote control strapped to his wrist.*) Been looking everywhere for that!

ALICE: (*Prompting him.*) You come in...

BUZZ points his finger like a gun at the TV, clutching his wrist with his free hand, pressing the remote control. The TV screen flashes on and off.

You come in the front...

BUZZ: "Hi! I'm your friendly neighbourhood bagman."

ALICE: And if I give the nod?

BUZZ: (*Briefly fazed.*) The nod?(*Catching her drift.*) The routine, man! Run the routine.

Marks the routine, doing his impression of a shaman.

"Hi, man. I'm Brujo, and this here's my blind lizard."

ALICE: What about the bag?

BUZZ: Medicine bag. Magic herb, root and bark.

ALICE: Don't forget –

BUZZ: "Don't forget the bag!" We done the bag. Okay? If that don't work we bring out the lizards.

ALICE: If we must.

BUZZ: The lizards with the stitched-up eyes.

ALICE: Thanks, Buzz. That'll do. You got the map?

BUZZ checks his jacket, brings out a folded map, shows her.

BUZZ: What if he don't drink coffee?

ALICE: That's my problem.

Door-bell rings. TV screen shows CROWE, out in the street, staring suspiciously at the security camera.

ALICE: (*Speaking into intercom.*) Hi, Crowe! Come on down. (*Pushes a button.*)

BUZZ: Don't forget what I said. I'll be upstairs if–

ALICE: You just worry about keeping your act together. Oh, and Buzz. Do me a favour. No more spliffs.

BUZZ: Safe. (*Walks over to the wall.*) All yours, babes.

Disappears through the wall. Pause. CROWE appears outside the cell-door, dressed in black, carrying an attaché case.

CROWE: Hi, Alice.

ALICE: Hi, Crowe. How you doin'?

Unlocks the door to let him in.

CROWE: Talk about security!

ALICE: (*Shrugs.*) Why make it easy for them?

CROWE: (*Scans the room.*) Looks like you got yourself the best front in town.

ALICE: Bucket-shop.

CROWE: Must be at least ten others in the building.

ALICE: For all I know, we all sell the same ticket.

CROWE: You always operate from here?

ALICE: Appointment only.

CROWE: You don't trust the customers?

ALICE: What they don't know can't hurt them.

Casually making for the coffee-machine.

Coffee?

CROWE: Uh, no thanks. I can't stay.

ALICE: You got time. I made some fresh.

CROWE: Well, why not? Thanks. Black, no sugar.

Sits on the couch, cradling his black attaché case, surveying the room. ALICE pours two cups of coffee, handing CROWE the cup doctored by Buzz.

Got to hand it to you. Perfect front. Plus a neat way to launder a lot of money. Thirty round trips to Guatemala.

ALICE offers him a cigarette.

No thanks. Trying to give up.

ALICE lights her own cigarette and walks back to sit behind her desk. She shuffles her papers, playing the travel agent.

ALICE: We placed your reservation. Block booking.

CROWE: (*Frowns.*) Reservation? I'm er... I'm here to collect the tickets.

ALICE: It's all arranged.

CROWE: Thirty tickets. Four thousand a ticket? (*She nods.*) Not exactly bargain basement!

ALICE: I thought we'd agreed terms.

CROWE: Whose terms?

ALICE: Our terms. The terms we agreed.

CROWE: (*Gets up, coming up close to her, lowering his voice.*) You think this place is wired?

ALICE: (*Laughs.*) What do they care? I'm small fry.

CROWE: Okay, so... We're talking Ice. Rock. Crystal.

ALICE: The best.

CROWE: Four thousand a key.

ALICE: Assuming you still want thirty.

CROWE: Hundred and twenty grand! Not exactly small time.

ALICE: You must live a sheltered life. The big players deal in millions.

CROWE: Your source, you mean?

ALICE: This is an exception. I'm doing it as a favour.

CROWE: I am grateful, believe me. (*Pause.*) You must have very good connections.

ALICE: That's my cut.

CROWE: I don't begrudge you, but I like to know I'm buying close to the source.

ALICE: Couldn't be closer.

CROWE: To the Iceman? (*Off ALICE's stare.*) What?

ALICE: I've a feeling we've met before.

CROWE: (*Puzzled.*) We have. I mean, we've done a couple of deals.

ALICE: Before that.

CROWE: (*Stares at her.*) Nah! Never forget a face. You might've seen me at one of Kate's raves. I mean, before she introduced us –

ALICE: Oh, man, don't talk to me about Speedy Kate! Saw her the other night. Nyak-nyak-nyak-nyak-nyak! – can't understand a fucking word she's saying. (*They laugh.*) No, way before that.

CROWE: (*Shrugs.*) So... Shall we get down to business?

Gets up and puts the attaché case on the desk, opening it to reveal stacked wads of bank-notes. She nods, impressed.

Hundred and twenty grand. Used bank-notes. Untraceable. (*Pause.*) Well? Aren't you going to count it?

ALICE: I trust you.

CROWE: For one twenty K? At least take a look at it! For all you know it could be mickey-mouse money. I mean, I might smell something, you know?

ALICE: (*Laughs.*) A rat. That's what people smell isn't it. Rats? Paranoia, man. Now. Let's see... (*Riffles a wad, extracts a bank-note, holding it up to the light.*) Looks okay to me.

CROWE: Okay. (*Pause.*) So... The tickets.

ALICE: Ah, yes! The tickets haven't arrived yet.

CROWE: Well, where the fuck are they?

ALICE: No problem. It's a simple procedure. I check the payment, make one phone-call –

CROWE: What if your phone's bugged?

ALICE: We've been through that. Anyway, we use a code.

CROWE: Codes get cracked. These crackhead and smackhead codes – tickets and books and slices of cakes – who the fuck do you think you're fooling? You said you could deliver –

ALICE: What's your problem, man? You expect me to front a thirty kilo Ice deal? No way! On a deal this size, I have to cover my ass.

CROWE: What about my fucking ass?

ALICE: What about it? Fucking uptight-ass, man!

CROWE gets up, giving the office the once-over, using a brochure for emphasis.

CROWE: This place is all front, right? Short-let in someone else's name. I'm supposed to hand over one twenty K. and sit around looking at – holiday brochures, waiting for you to –

ALICE: (*Laughs.*) I'm not going to walk your money. I'm not going anywhere. I stay here. With you.

CROWE: But –

ALICE: You think I collect?

CROWE: I thought you said –

ALICE: They deliver.

CROWE: So... Money stays here.

ALICE: One phone call.

CROWE: That's alright then. (*Pause.*) So make it.

ALICE: (*Glances at her watch.*) I have to call at a pre-arranged time.

CROWE: And I'm supposed to sit here like a – (*Checks himself.*) I'm sorry. I'm a bit edgy. So when? (*Once again aware of her scrutiny.*) Now what?

ALICE: (*With a start of sudden recognition.*) I know!

CROWE: (*On guard.*) What?

ALICE: North Wales. The acid factory. Must be about what? – ten years ago. There was a big party, everyone doing A. and E. and dancing round a bonfire. Remember? We were both well out of it but... It was you, wasn't it?

CROWE: (*Evasively.*) You know those Welsh acid parties... All blur into one big... blur!

ALICE: Not for me.

CROWE: No?

ALICE: No, for me, each one – crystal clear.

CROWE: Did we fuck?

ALICE: Not that I recall. (*CROWE graciously acknowledges her put-down with a smile.*) We may have hugged.

CROWE: (*Laughing.*) Hugged?

ALICE: As I recall it was quite a huggy scene.

CROWE: Those Welsh hippies, huh? Well maybe there was something in it. Maybe we could both do with a hug right now. (*Offers to hug her.*) I mean there's no law says we have to behave like evil drug-dealers.

ALICE: I don't think I'm ready to hug you just yet.

CROWE: (*Shrugs.*) Suit yourself.

ALICE: Maybe later, when I get to know you.

CROWE: But – I thought you said –

ALICE: I never said I knew you.

CROWE: Oh. Okay. Only where do I get this sneaky feeling you're coming on to me?

ALICE: (*Beat, smiles.*) No. What I said was –

CROWE: We've met before.

ALICE: Precisely.

CROWE: And hugged.

ALICE: Maybe. I do remember talking to you.

CROWE: And talked! About what?

ALICE: Dunno... Something about – yeah... Multiple personalities!

CROWE: (*Laughing, incredulous.*) We talked about what?

ALICE: Is it possible to live more than one life in any given time-frame.

CROWE: Jesus! That's some memory you've got there! Wait... (*Bluffing.*) I remember. (*Laughs.*) Far out! But, I mean, we're talking way back. I'd never've recognised you.

ALICE: I've changed. So have you.

CROWE: Well, thank God we didn't fuck!

ALICE: No. We didn't fuck. Fucking was not on the agenda that night.

CROWE: I mean forget-a-face is one thing, but to forget a body like... (*Gestures approvingly, intending a compliment.*)

ALICE: The agenda was double lives. Dual personalities. And you said, I remember distinctly, that if two lives ever came together, in the same space and time, that one of them would have to die.

CROWE: I said that? I must've been out of my skull!

ALICE: We both were. (*They laugh.*)

CROWE: (*Suddenly on guard.*) So how come you remember?

ALICE: What?

CROWE: What I said. If you were out of your brains...

ALICE: Don't know... Must've stuck in my mind.

CROWE: Or maybe you imagined it.

ALICE: Well, maybe...

CROWE: Hallucinated.

ALICE: It's possible. (*Awkward pause.*)

CROWE: When are you going to make that call?

ALICE: (*Glancing at her watch.*) Ten minutes.

CROWE: And how long they take to deliver?

ALICE: Depends on the traffic. Twenty minutes, half an hour... There's a sample.

Hands him the bag of Ice crystals. CROWE opens the bag, takes out one of the crystals, holding it up to the light.

CROWE: Looks good.

Licks his finger, tasting it.

Mind if I kick up a little freeze?

ALICE: You mean "cook?" Cook up a freeze.

CROWE: Cook. Kick. Cock. Who cares?

ALICE: You want to sample? Thirty keys in the balance and you want to stiff your brains on Ice?

CROWE: I can handle it.

ALICE: That's what they all say.

CROWE: Look, it's no big deal. Before I part with this kind of money, I want to check the quality.

ALICE: (*Shrugs.*) They're your brains. You want to cock up a freeze? You go right ahead, honey.

ALICE hands CROWE a pipe. He prepares a chip off the crystal.

CROWE: You guys usually insist I sample the goods.

ALICE: "Us guys"? What sort of guys are we?

CROWE: You'd trust a customer didn't use?

She shrugs. He applies a flame to the pipe, inhales, closes his eyes, savouring the rush. Offers her the pipe. She shakes her head.

No?

ALICE: No way, José. You know what that stuff is?

CROWE: Cracked speed. Ice, man! Fastest rush on earth.

ALICE: Methedrine, man! Cheapest, dirtiest speed on the street. Now they've cracked it up –

CROWE: Feel free to criticize, sweetheart. You only sell the stuff.

ALICE: Someone has to. Look, if it'll make you feel more relaxed, I'll skin up a joint. Okay?

CROWE: You do that. Yes. To see you roll a little number would make me feel much more relaxed right now.

ALICE: No problem.

Opens the drawer, takes out rizlas and hashish, starts rolling a joint.

Like I said, I don't deal Ice. Now, if you want the best black west of Katmandu, few tabs of A. or E. –

CROWE: You said you had a direct line to the Iceman.

ALICE: I told you – it's a one-off. Look, man, I'm doing you a fucking favour. I don't need the hassle. Back off! Okay?

CROWE: Okay. Okay. No big deal.

Wanders upstage, idly picking up the mirror-glass bird.

What the fuck is this?

ALICE: Glass-work. Quetzal bird. Custom-made. Careful! Cost me an arm and a leg.

CROWE: What's this wire plugged in the back?

ALICE: Oh... Yeah, it's er... It's meant to light up. The bulb's fucked.

CROWE examines the bird more closely, staring at his broken reflection in the mirrors. ALICE chatters nervously, trying to distract him.

Yes. It's a bird. Quetzal. We get all our brochures from the Guatemalan tourist board. It's their national symbol. Montezuma – you know, the Aztecs? – he gave Cortes a headdress of quetzal feathers. A gift. Whereupon our noble conquistador proceeds to ice the Aztecs and steal their keys to the Other Side – you know, the vision world where all good trippers go? What gets me is why anyone who's done acid would want to go chasing cheap thrills on cracked Ice.

CROWE puts the bird back on the shelf, in a different position.

CROWE: Look... No-one's denying... Ice can really screw you up if you don't know how to handle it. Obviously it fucks up your sleep rhythm.

ALICE: You lose your appetite.

CROWE: Lose a little weight.

ALICE: Your teeth rot. You look like shit!

CROWE: Looks aren't everything. I'm saying, it's not going to kill you.

ALICE: Could get you killed, or so wired you'll ice anyone who gets in your way. You seen what it's like out there? "You dissin' me, man?" Bangbangbang! Stiffheads packing fucking Uzis! Man, that's all we need!

CROWE: I suppose it does incite a certain amount of antisocial behaviour. (*Off her derisive laugh.*) So? You going to outlaw booze? Look. It's not addictive, not physically.

ALICE: Nor is crack. You know what it costs to support a crack habit?

CROWE: Depends... Fifty... Hundred...

ALICE: A day! Where do you get that kind of money?

CROWE: We can talk about a psychological dependence.

ALICE: Physical? Psychological? What's the fucking difference?

CROWE: So. Why dirty your fingers?

ALICE has no answer to this. She finishes rolling, lights the joint.

CROWE: Okay. Here's what we do. You call your source. You tell him all about me.

ALICE: What? Over my bugged phone? (*Takes a hit.*)

CROWE: Use one of your codes. Your cousin wants to see his book collection.

ALICE laughs, coughs, splutters.

Cut out the middleman. Woman. Okay okay, you want your cut, right? Finder's fee. Fine, but I mean, come on! You say you're not into it. You don't even use. You can't afford to front the deal, so we have to play this weird waiting game. Who needs it? Put me in touch with the Iceman. I'll take it from there.

ALICE: No way, José!

CROWE: Look... All I'm asking is an introduction... I need to score on a regular basis.

ALICE: Where do you put it, Crowe? It can't all be for personal consumption.

CROWE: I deal enough to support my habit.

ALICE: Thirty kilos! That's one hell of a habit.

CROWE: What's that to you?

ALICE: Nothing... Just curious.

CROWE: Like you said, it has to come from somewhere. Either you deal or you shake people down.

ALICE: So much hassle – for what? Half-hour stiffed out your brains?

CROWE: You thank your lucky stars you're dealing with a dealer.

ALICE: Low-grade high, man!

ALICE offers CROWE the joint. He shakes his head disparagingly.

CROWE: Each to his own, man. Horses for courses. Ever do horse?

ALICE: You must be joking! I've seen what that shit does to people.

CROWE: You seen plenty. Maybe too much.

ALICE: Too much?

CROWE: For your own good.

The phone rings. ALICE answers it.

ALICE: Quetzal travel... (*Listens.*) Yes... When do you want to go? (*Scribbles on a pad.*) Hmm-hmm... Let's see... I can get you two seats on a charter to Cancun on the 23rd...

CROWE: Jesus! (*Helps himself to more coffee. Lights a cigarette.*)

ALICE: (*On the phone.*) Four hundred and seventy nine...
We can leave the return open... Are you paying by
credit card? Well, I can hold the tickets for three days.
If you put a cheque in the post or... No, not today. The
office is closed. We're only taking telephone bookings.
You could call in tomorrow. We're open 9 till 5...
Fine... You're welcome. Bye... (*Puts down the phone.*)

CROWE: Sounds like business is booming.

She smiles, giving nothing away.

So... How's about it?

ALICE: Hmm?

CROWE: You help me make the connection.

ALICE: Forget it. Look, man, the minute I stop protecting my source, I'm fucked! I mean, for all I know,
you could be a fucking nark.

CROWE: A narc! Me? (*As cod copper.*) "Excuse me, sir, I
have reason to believe you can er... turn me on."

ALICE: I hear they've sharpened up their act.

CROWE: A copper stiffed on Ice?

ALICE: Copper's nark. Would you know if you saw one?

CROWE: Too right! Don't know who you're dealing
with, these days. I could say the same about you. (*She
shrugs.*) So. We're paranoid. Can you blame us? When
they can kick down your door in the middle of the night,
wave a gun in your face, freeze your assets – just on
suspicion! Fucking police state! And for what? I know of
only one person who died as a direct result of drugs he
scored from me. Jesus! Compared to Marlboro Man I'm
Mother fucking Theresa!

ALICE: Don't try to make sense of the drug laws. You
get the same time for dealing acid you'd get for
pushing smack. It's almost an incentive.

CROWE: It is. Exactly! That's exactly what it is!

ALICE: (*A beat.*) How do you mean?

CROWE: They deliberately created the drug problem. They are the fucking problem.

ALICE: "They"? Who's they?

CROWE: (*Conspiratorially.*) Acid tests?

ALICE: (*Catching his drift.*) Before my time.

CROWE: Operation Mind Control. Even got some tart to spike the johns – they'd film the poor fucks coming apart, all shot through two-way mirrors – psychedelic peepshows! Acid, speed, you name it – hundred thirty nine drugs secretly tested by the CIA – chemical weapons, okay? – all targeted at quote subversive elements unquote –

ALICE: What do you expect? CIA handing out free acid? The freaks couldn't believe their luck! They were queuing up to volunteer.

CROWE: Think about it! Blacks. Prisoners. Prostitutes.

ALICE: Speedy Kate reckons they did the same with the Aids virus.

CROWE: Who's to say they didn't? What the fuck do we know?

Under the influence of the Ice, he has become more assertive. He holds ALICE's gaze, demanding her undivided attention.

Only this time they fucked-up, right? The acid tests blew up in their faces. They set out to control us and end up blowing our minds.

ALICE: Come on, man! This is ancient history!

CROWE: Whose history? History made in a TV studio?

ALICE: You're old enough to remember.

CROWE: If you remember, you weren't there.

ALICE: And what about love?

CROWE: What about it?

ALICE: I thought it was all you needed.

CROWE: And maybe it was – before it got ripped and – adulterated with fear and *need* and – packaged like some new all-purpose consumer drug.

A blast of music makes them both jump.

CROWE: What the fuck!

ALICE: Oh shit! It's the guys upstairs in the recording studio.

CROWE: Recording studio? It's coming from in here.

ALICE: No. That's your head, man. That's the Ice. (*Shouting.*) Shut the fuck up! (*Music stops.*) I'm sorry. You were saying?

CROWE: (*Disorientated.*) Recording studio?

ALICE: (*Prompting him.*) So it's like the CIA accidentally opens a window and then spends the next thirty years trying to shut it.

CROWE: I'm saying... The order was given. "Shut. Down. Shut them down. Fuck with the acid. Cut it with smack, speed, strychnine." You could taste it, in your teeth. And the stomach cramps on the comedown.

ALICE: Cheapskate dealers cutting their stash.

CROWE: With strychnine?

ALICE: Paranoia.

CROWE: It was happening. I've seen the list.

ALICE: List? What sort of list?

CROWE: Hit list. (*Giggles.*) The hundred and thirty nine steps. Street-acid? I tell you, kids today, don't know what they're dropping.

ALICE: You don't need the CIA to explain that. Speedy Kate made a fortune selling malaria pills at one of her raves – twenty quid a hit.

CROWE: You see? Easy. You'd convince yourself that only E. could taste that bad.

ALICE: So? What are we saying? Speedy Kate is working for the CIA?

CROWE: We're saying how to create a drug problem. Shut down the acid. Burn the dope-fields. Flood the streets with cheap heroin, flown in direct from South East Asia...

ALICE: Why, man? Why go to all that hassle?

CROWE: Control.

ALICE: Oh! Yeah. Right.

CROWE: Junkie's entire life revolves around the next fix. You hold the key to the medicine cabinet, you control that junkie absolutely.

ALICE: Burroughs freak, huh?

CROWE: Huh?

ALICE: He's been saying that for the last thirty years.

CROWE: Great minds... So? What are you saying?

ALICE: Just checking your sources.

CROWE: So? Some famous junkie has a copyright on the truth? What do you expect? Last days of the Twentieth Century... Everything worth saying or doing has been said and done. There isn't an original thought left in the universe.

ALICE: (*Smiles.*) Even that thought isn't original.

CROWE: So what do we do? We get Iced! Go ahead, man, stack us in the fridge. Thaw us out when you got something new to show us.

Paces restlessly.

Speaking of sources...

ALICE: I haven't forgotten. (*Glances at her watch.*) Three minutes.

CROWE paces, stops, staring at the framed poster.

Aztec calendar.

CROWE: There's control for you! Uncle Bill reckoned they could've taught the CIA a thing or two.

ALICE: Before or after they killed the Kennedys? Come on, man. You don't believe this conspiracy bullshit!

CROWE: You got a better theory? We've been fighting the war on drugs for the last thirty years, for what? The harder we fight it, the worse it gets. The drugs get dirtier –

ALICE: Because people are stupid and greedy. So dealers start cutting their stash with shit. Junkies make better customers –

CROWE: (*Ranting.*) Better headlines. Gang wars. ODs. Junkies sharing dirty needles – there's one for Speedy Kate! Don't you see how it plays into their hands? It's all a fucking smokescreen!

ALICE: Certainly they'll use it to push for more police powers –

CROWE: Civil rights? We piss in their mouth! National sovereignty? We'll take out Colombia.

ALICE: But if you're seriously suggesting someone took the trouble to sit down and dream up –

CROWE: Death to the drug barons! Everything permitted! War on drugs? It's one big fucking sideshow!

He stops in his tracks, staring in amazement as a section of the wall opens. Enter BUZZ, evidently embarrassed. ALICE gives him a look that could kill.

BUZZ: Er... Sorry to interrupt.

ALICE: (*Sighs, to CROWE.*) This is Buzz, my er – partner.

CROWE: Bugs?

BUZZ: Buzzzzzzz, man! Buzz-buzz. No bugs on me, man. And you are?

CROWE: Crowe.

BUZZ: Crow. Come to score a set of wings.

CROWE: Crowe. With an E.

BUZZ: Take my advice, man, drop the E. The E take you higher. Crowe with an E, you my man!

CROWE: So... She keeps you stashed in the wall?

BUZZ: Yeah, man, in case of emergency. (*To ALICE.*) Between you and me, babes, the big picture is fucked. Who's been fucking with my fit-up?

ALICE: (*Furious.*) Fuck you, Buzz!

BUZZ: Sure, babes, but I'm stewing in there, you know? Got some great shots of the shelving. Not going to win any prizes with that. Tried to reach you on the airwaves, but you don't read me.

ALICE: You want to screw the entire package?

BUZZ: Just thought I'd better let you know, man. As it stands, ain't worth jack-shit.

CROWE: What the set is this fuck-up, anyway?

ALICE: (*Aside to BUZZ.*) Verbal dysfunction.

BUZZ: (*To CROWE.*) Don't mind me, man. I'm not even here.

ALICE: (*To BUZZ, angrily.*) You! Sit down and shut the fuck up. (*To CROWE, apologetically.*) Stiffheads!

CROWE: What's all this about "big pictures".

ALICE: Another fucking conspiracy freak. Which is why I don't want the two of yous to get talking.

BUZZ: Sorry, Sylvia...

ALICE: Alice.

BUZZ: Alice, but no use complaining when you see what we haven't got.

ALICE: (*To CROWE.*) See what happens? Your brain freezes up.

CROWE: Not if you know how to use it.

BUZZ: True, man. Use it to check the levels.

CROWE: Exactly. You want to take a fix on something –

ALICE: Get.

CROWE: What?

ALICE: You "get" a fix on something. You "take", or "have" a fix, as in junk. You see, apart from anything else, it completely fucks up your grammar.

BUZZ wanders over to polish the mirror-glass bird with his handkerchief, casually readjusting its position on the shelf.

CROWE: (*Joining him.*) What you doing?

BUZZ: The glass-work, man. Dusting the glass-work. (*Holding the jagged mirrors up to his face.*) Is a crow, man. See? The crow in the mirror.

CROWE: What's this wire for.

BUZZ: Wire, man?

CROWE: (*Shows him the wire plugged into the back of the glass bird.*) What do you call this?

ALICE: I told you. It's a light.

BUZZ: Yeah. Right... Yeah. The bulb's fucked... (*To ALICE.*) Hey, look, babes, how are we going to do the bagman?

ALICE: We don't. You've fucked it, haven't you?

CROWE: Fucked what?

ALICE: The light. Leave it to me, Buzz. (*To CROWE.*) This man's a fucking mad alchemist, walking laboratory. He's personally test-driven every known chemical. In the process most of his brains've turned to mush.

BUZZ: Thanks, bitch!

ALICE: Man's a fucking liability, but do I kick him out on the street. No way! He's my partner, and I'll stand by him, even when he can't even remember my fucking name...

BUZZ: Okay, babes. Man don't want to know about that.

ALICE: (*Looks at her watch.*) It's time.

Picks up the phone, dials.

CROWE: Ask him.

ALICE: About what?

CROWE: Making contact.

ALICE: Well, sure, I'll try. Can't promise.

CROWE: Sure... But you will tell him, about me...

ALICE: (*Speaking on the phone.*) Hi, angel. It's me. I was thinking of coming round to see you... Did you talk to her? (*Listens.*) Well I think it's about time you told her the truth. Oh. You did. And? (*Listens.*) She what? Heavy! (*Listens.*) Yeah, I know. Always is when there's kids involved.

CROWE: (*Whispers.*) Ask him.

ALICE: (*Nods impatiently, speaking on the phone.*) I understand... Look, I don't want a heavy heart-to-heart. Be good to see you, that's all. Okay? (*Listens.*) Love you too... Bye.

Puts down phone.

ALICE: Change of plan. Iceman can't deliver. Buzz, he wants you to collect.

BUZZ: No problem.

CROWE: What about me?

ALICE: What about you?

CROWE: Will he see me?

ALICE: Maybe.

CROWE: When?

ALICE: When I've checked you out.

CROWE: How long will that take?

ALICE: As long as it takes. You score from me on a regular basis... Not tonight, anyhow.

CROWE: You didn't even ask him.

ALICE: Of course I did. I told you, we use a code.

CROWE: Oh yeah? So what did you say to him? I didn't hear anything about introductions.

ALICE: The stuff about his wife.

CROWE: You asked if he'd spoken to her.

ALICE: Means I've got a client wants to meet him.

CROWE: And?

ALICE: He said it was difficult. She's going through a bad patch. Says if he doesn't stop seeing me, she's going to take custody... I don't have to explain that, huh? (*CROWE smiles doubtfully.*) The kids means he wants Buzz to collect.

CROWE: And the heart-to-heart?

ALICE: I confirm the change of plan.

CROWE: Nice. Very nice. For all I know you could be setting up a sting.

ALICE: You have to take my word for it.

CROWE: Seems I have no choice.

ALICE: That's what it's all about, eh Crowe?

CROWE: What is what all about?

ALICE: Trying to crack each other's codes. The basis of all human relationships.

CROWE: (*Pause.*) So how come he can go but not me?

ALICE: He's known.

CROWE: Uh-huh? (*To BUZZ.*) So you know what's his name?

ALICE: (*To BUZZ.*) Don't answer that. He's fishing... Okay, Buzz. You know the routine...

BUZZ: Out the back...

ALICE: I don't need to hear it. Just do it.

BUZZ: Right. (*Makes to leave, hesitates.*) Er... Do I still get to eat the pizza?

ALICE: Of course. And don't forget –

BUZZ: "Don't forget the bag!" (*Pulls a face at CROWE, picking up his attaché case.*)

CROWE: Hey! Where you going with that?

BUZZ: I thought this was the loot.

CROWE: Yeah! Mine!

BUZZ: Yeah, well you've got to pay for it, right.

CROWE: I'm supposed to trust some burnt-out dopefiend–

ALICE: Careful, man. I can bad-mouth him all I want, but you try it, you are dead, man! Dead!

CROWE: I'm supposed to hand over one twenty K. for him to schlep across town.

BUZZ: Who says it's across town?

ALICE: Okay, Buzz.

BUZZ: Who's to say it's not just –

ALICE: Okay, Buzz, just do it.

BUZZ: It's done. (*Makes to leave.*)

CROWE: Hey, hey! Wait a minute. What's this "eat a pizza" number. You're going to some pizzeria with my hundred and twenty –

ALICE: Relax, Crowe. That's the meet.

CROWE: With the Iceman?

BUZZ: Bagman.

CROWE: No way, man!

ALICE: What d'you mean no?

CROWE: What do you take me for? Buzz walks out that's the last we see of him. What am I going to do? Call the cops? Tell them I got ripped off on a thirty kilo drug deal?

BUZZ: Why would we risk the hassle? We've got Ice in the fridge.

CROWE: But not thirty kilos, as agreed.

ALICE: You're too stiffed to remember what we agreed. Anyway, what difference does it make if the Ice is here or waiting in some pizzeria?

CROWE: (*Spelling it out in simple gestures.*) Here's the money. Here's the Ice.

ALICE: Look, Crowe, if I wanted to burn you, I could have Buzz pull a gun on you. Simple.

BUZZ: Don't take a gun. I could apply sudden pressure to any one of forty points on your body which would leave you unable to speak or write or otherwise communicate what had been done to you.

Tense pause.

ALICE: You see, Crowe, you have to trust people.

CROWE: True.

They all laugh, with a show of relaxing.

ALICE: (*Looks at her watch.*) Time ticking away. If he don't go soon, he'll miss his connection.

BUZZ: True. The Man wait for no man.

CROWE: Okay. (*To BUZZ.*) But she stays with me. I've got a few pressure points of my own. You read me?

BUZZ: No sweat, man. I get back, what say you and me cook up a little freeze?

CROWE: Sounds good, Buzz. Be quick. Be careful.

ALICE: It's okay. Even stiffheads can still run their old routines, right, Buzz? (*Unlocks cell-door.*)

BUZZ: Safe, man.

Exit BUZZ.

ALICE locks the door behind him. Awkward pause.

CROWE: Anything else up your sleeve?

ALICE: How do you mean?

CROWE: Coded phone calls. Special delivery. Waiting around for Buzz to eat his pizza... I mean, can you blame me?

ALICE: No, I don't blame you. Not in the least. Why should blame even enter our relationship? What can I say? Me and Buzz – we're well dodgy – Operation Shoestring.

CROWE: (*Wrong-footed by her frank admission.*) Even so... Takes time to put-up a front like this. (*Off her laugh.*) No. There must be other levels.

ALICE: I mean, fuck, man – even I don't buy it!

CROWE stares at her, bemused.

Question is, why did you?

CROWE: What d'you mean? You just talked me into it.

ALICE: You didn't take much convincing.

CROWE: Did I have a choice?

ALICE: Of course!

CROWE: You're not as dodgy as you like to think. (*Laughs.*) I mean, come on! Why would any sane human being set themselves up to get burnt?

ALICE: Nothing personal, but addiction to a drug like Ice is hardly a question of sanity.

CROWE: Who says I'm addicted?

ALICE: You did.

CROWE: I don't remember...

ALICE: I do, quite distinctly.

CROWE: Yeah, well, you remember conversations that may or may not have taken place under the influence of LSD.

Begins distractedly leafing through a holiday brochure.

ALICE: (*Staring at him.*) I'm sure it was you.

CROWE: Could've been. Once upon a time, in another life. You wouldn't've been Alice then, would you? You could have been – Sylvia?

ALICE: You know they got busted.

CROWE seems to be having some trouble focusing. He holds the brochure at arms length, then brings it close to his face.

CROWE: (*Distractedly.*) Who?

ALICE: The Welsh hippies.

CROWE: Yeah... Heavy.

ALICE: Couple of weeks later.

CROWE: Later than what?

ALICE: The party. The night we met.

CROWE: Oh, yeah... Like I said, I'm terrible with faces.

ALICE: No, what you said was "I never forget a face". Faces you never forget. Isn't that a symptom? You lose awareness of contradictory thoughts and behaviour.

CROWE: Since when are you such an expert in the pathology of Ice?

ALICE: How long have you been using?

CROWE: Couple months, on and off... I can control it. Bet you're a real pain in the ass to live with.

ALICE: So what's the kick?

CROWE: The kick, sweetie, is one mule-kick mother of all rushes, makes you feel like you can fuck the whole world and then come! The kick is the street's all-purpose painkiller. Man, when those receptors ice up, you won't feel a thing.

ALICE: Stiffed!

CROWE: The big freeze. White as snow, hard as horse. Neutral screen. You are the projectionist. You are what you project.

ALICE: Take it from me, Crowe, you're projecting a lot more than you think.

CROWE: Don't believe everything you hear. Never saw a stiffhead die of frostbite. I'd say –

ALICE: I'd say you've been using longer than you care to admit.

CROWE: On what do you base that observation?

ALICE: There are tests.

CROWE: Tests?

ALICE: To determine the extent of the damage.

CROWE: Is that what's going on here?

ALICE: Oh, yes. I'd say, a test is definitely being undergone, wouldn't you?

CROWE: Any results?

ALICE: Inconclusive.

CROWE, sweating, takes off his coat, draping it on the chair.

CROWE: For what?

ALICE: What?

CROWE: For what am I being tested?

ALICE: I was hoping you could tell me.

CROWE: (*Laughs, incredulous.*) Jesus! I don't know if I'll be doing business with you again. You come to cop, you don't expect an interrogation.

ALICE: (*Laughs.*) Did I hear you right? "Come to cop?" Did you really say that?

CROWE: Yeah! You know. Score!

ALICE: I know, but don't you see? It's your choice of words, curiously old-fashioned. You see, if you interpret it literally, when you "come to cop" an interrogation is exactly what you expect.

CROWE: What are you trying to pull?

ALICE: Freudian slip. No, not Freudian. Reichian. Reichian slip.

CROWE takes a gulp of coffee. His arm shakes, spilling coffee on his shirt.

Careful, man – fuck! Wait. I'll get a cloth.

ALICE rummages in the bottom-drawer of the filing cabinet, brings out a wet cloth.

CROWE: It's okay. Won't stain...

ALICE: No. Here. (*Dabbing at his shirt.*) See what I mean, man? Message from your nervous system. You receive messages?

CROWE: Messages?

ALICE: Yeah, you know... TV, radio... Messages... From the other side...

Rubs the stain on his shirt. He seems ill-at-ease with this sudden intimacy.

You know... When you listen very hard to some ordinary sound – say water filling a cistern, under the water you'll sometimes hear voices. Sometimes they tell you what to do.

CROWE: You're asking was I programmed?

ALICE: Subliminal criminals.

CROWE: You trying to outweird me?

ALICE is wiping the coffee stain, methodically working her way down the shirt. CROWE tenses.

ALICE: Relax, man! I'm not going to rape you. Hey, what's this under your shirt?

CROWE flinches, knocking her away, almost losing his balance.

CROWE: (*Awkwardly.*) I... I'm sorry.

ALICE: (*Throws down the rag, sits on the couch.*) It's people like you give drugs a bad name. I don't know, man. If someone had deliberately set out to fuck you up –

CROWE: Maybe they did. Maybe that's the one fact you don't want to face.

ALICE: Hmm?

CROWE joins her on the couch, eerily calm and collected.

CROWE: You think it's an accident I get hooked? Uh-huh! All part of the plan.

ALICE: And what part do you play? Where do you fit in?

CROWE: I'm the fat lady. Gimme a shot and I'll sing. I knew too much. An order was given.

ALICE: To get you hooked? Get you strung out on Ice.

CROWE: Not Ice, man! How many times? You don't get hooked on Ice. Smack! Scag! Horse! Heroin.

ALICE: Shit! (*Pause.*) Why not just rub you out?

CROWE: An eye for an eye. Their idea of a joke.

ALICE: What's the joke? What's so funny about junkies?

CROWE: Take me to the edge. Can't make me jump. That's where they fucked up. They'll pay...

ALICE: Shit, man, are you ever weird! I had every right to take precautions. Who are these people?

CROWE: Don't expect them to come wearing badges.They look just like me and you. They move among us and we don't even see them. But we will... see and know them for what they are.

ALICE: Cut the spooky tales, man. What are they? Nazis? Aliens? Prominent members of the British royal family? Come on, man, put up or shut up.

CROWE: Too late. My lips are iced.

Pause.

ALICE: I don't get it.

CROWE: What do you not get?

ALICE: The joke. Why should anyone deliberately set out to get you addicted?

CROWE: Shut me down.

ALICE: I can think of more dependable ways. "An eye for an eye". Where's the punchline? Unless...

CROWE: Unless?

ALICE: You're a nark.

CROWE laughs, a bit too loud.

That would be eye for eye. If I found out you were a nark, I'd spike you myself! Slip you some bad acid, one way ticket to the Aztec snake-pit!

CROWE: Nark? As in "rat"? Stool-pigeon? "Grass in the park"?

ALICE: Be just like a nark to dream up some paranoid conspiracy at his own expense. Now there's a fucking punchline! He turns up at the Welsh farmhouse. Before you can say "hea-vy!" – the hippies get busted!

CROWE: Now who's paranoid?

ALICE: What you got taped to your stomach? Transmitter?

CROWE, wrong-footed, smiles ruefully.

How long do you take to burn down your dealer? How long have I got, Crowe?

CROWE: Until you blow my cover.

He has completely recovered his composure, dropping his "addict cover" to assume the authoritative manner of a street-wise nar p- cotics officer.

Bad move, sweetie. Used up your time too fast. Time just ran out.

ALICE: (*Laughing nervously.*) Come on, man! I was winding you up.

CROWE: (*Laughs.*) A narc, me? Too fucking right! That's narc with a C. As in plain-clothes. Undercover. Narcotics agent.

ALICE: (*Lamely.*) It was a joke.

CROWE: Well, then, maybe, if we both have a good laugh about it, maybe it'll all be all right.

Pause. He lets it sink in.

ALICE: So... I'm busted.

CROWE: So it would seem.

Pause.

ALICE: Well fuck me!

Sound of a police siren in the street, coming closer, louder.

Blackout.

End of Act One

ACT TWO

The action continues: ALICE hunched on the couch, in shock; CROWE standing over her. Sound of the police siren outside, coming closer, louder.

ALICE: Fuck me!

The police siren recedes, fading. CROWE casually refills his coffee cup, biding his time.

Of all the stiffheads in London, I have to pick a fucking –

CROWE: We do the plucking.

He offers her a refill. She refuses, sulking.

Anyone who can shift a thirty kilo Icecap –

ALICE: Fuck you, man! You set me up. You were hassling everyone for a connection. I only agreed as a –

CROWE: As agreed! Greed! Greed.

ALICE: Go stiff yourself!

CROWE laughs, sitting behind the desk.

CROWE: You really bought my addict routine, eh? You think I want that shit in my veins? And when I cooked up a freeze? "Ah didn' inhale..." Basic training. Shoot it up your sleeve.

ALICE: I never bought it. (*Pause.*) You blew it, man.

CROWE: I don't think so.

ALICE: I saw right through you, narc.

CROWE: Won't do you any good. Only complicates matters.

Wanders over to the filing-cabinet, opens the top drawer, peers inside.

Well well well! What have we here?

Takes out a spoon, a dropper, and a hypodermic syringe.

Junkie's repair kit.

Placing the gear on the desk, he returns to delve into the drawer, taking out various bottles, phials and zip-lock bags.

My lucky day!

Piles the evidence on the desk. She does not react. He waits patiently.

Well?

ALICE: I don't have to say anything until I've spoken to my solicitor.

CROWE: May not come to that. There's still time.

ALICE: For what?

CROWE: For you. To... examine your options.

Offers her a cigarette. She shakes her head. He lights his own.

Look... We're not interested in you. It's the Man behind you we're after. The Iceman. (*Pause.*) That's how we work – do a few small-time deals, gain your confidence, then... We put in an order you can't afford to front. You put us in touch with your source. You see? – work our way up the pyramid. Or, in this case, the iceberg. (*Pause.*) Took a lot of climbing just to get to you. I had reason to believe I'd hit the jackpot.

ALICE: (*Shrugs.*) We all make mistakes.

CROWE: Thing is, I'm here to make an arrest. And you are dressed to fit the bill. I'd say we're looking at... ten years? Minimum.

Sips his coffee. She does not respond.

You're doing time, while the real criminals are kissing ass in the Masons' Lodge. You hear what I'm saying? Friends in high places. You want to do their time? Fuck them! Let them do their own fucking time!

ALICE: Is that an offer?

CROWE: You said yourself, you're small fry. Why waste time and money, when you could help us land a fucking great shark? You tell me everything you know about the Iceman, contacts, connections, codes, anything... Then when our friend Buzz returns, what say we all go pay him a visit?

ALICE: That's the deal? I set up the Man. You want me to walk in there and finger him?

CROWE: You show us where to find him. We do the rest.

ALICE: You think I'm crazy, man? He'll know who narked on him.

CROWE: We'll get you out before we make our move. That's a promise.

ALICE: No "witness for the prosecution"?

CROWE: Should be able to keep you out of it. Provided we obtain the necessary evidence.

ALICE: What if the cupboard is bare?

CROWE: (*Shrugs.*) Ways to fill it.

ALICE considers his proposition.

ALICE: No... You'd have to arrest me too. For my own protection. And even then? What? Plea bargain? He'll know I've done a deal.

CROWE: No problem. First we charge you, then we fuck with your statement, make sure your brief gets to see it. Case collapses. Happens all the time.

ALICE: You expect me to trust you? Fucking cop posing as an addict?

CROWE: Junkie's honour. We're good at fucking up the evidence. Got it down to a fine art. (*Pause.*)

ALICE: I'll have that cigarette now.

CROWE gives her a cigarette, lights it.

So... I help you bust the Iceman. You think that'll change anything? There'll always be someone waiting to take his place. You want to solve the drug problem? Lock up everyone under sixteen.

CROWE: Tell that to the politicians! Most coppers would probably agree with you. The pusher is replaceable. We take out the Iceman, we merely create a vacuum, which nature will abhor... (*Slyly.*) Which you... may find yourself well placed... to fill...

ALICE: (*Smiles warily.*) That's a concept.

CROWE: You could be... the replacement.

ALICE: Working for you?

CROWE: Straight split on the profits for as long as it lasts.

ALICE: And how long do you think I'd last?

CROWE: You'd have my protection.

ALICE: "Protection"? From what? My local drug squad?

CROWE: They need never know.

ALICE: Let's get this straight. You're offering to set me up as a big player?

CROWE: Why not? Perfect front! With Iceman out of the picture, you're the hottest act in town. We're dancing with the big boys. Take them out one by one. Take out. Take over.

ALICE: (*Unimpressed.*) Uh-huh? What else can you offer me? Face transplant?

CROWE: It can be arranged. (*Pause.*) Well?

ALICE: Why should I believe you? Eh? Everything you've told me up to now has been a lie. Why should I believe you are what you say you are? You don't look like a cop to me.

CROWE: That's the whole idea.

ALICE: Let's see your ID.

CROWE: You think I walk around with a sheriff's badge pinned to my vest? Come on! I'm in deep cover. Even my Control doesn't know who I really am.

ALICE: Your "Control"?

CROWE: My handler. We never meet in the flesh. I report into a camera. They process my face on computer. See? Can't even trust our own!

ALICE: So like you could have two coppers posing as dealers, each one trying to bust the other.

CROWE: Happens all the time. But what if one of the coppers is bent? How do you know which is which? Huh? That's what this case is all about.

ALICE: Bent coppers? Well, nothing personal, man, but I'd say I'm looking at a prime suspect. Here's one copper just made me an offer I can't refuse.

CROWE: Takes one to catch one. (*Confidentially.*) We're talking about an experienced undercover agent, someone who knows how to cover his tracks. I have to get inside his head – habits, tradecraft, fire with fire... Oh, he's devious, but I know how to smoke him out.

ALICE: Chickenshit, man! I ask you to establish your identity, you proceed to cannibalise your own cover story. For fuck's sake, what you trying to sell me? The drug conspiracy – suddenly it's all true again? You're switching tracks so fast I don't know what the fuck –

Sees CROWE unbuttoning his shirt.

What the fuck do you think you're doing?

CROWE: Show you my wiring.

Pulls back his shirt to reveal a battery pack taped to his stomach with a wire trailing up to one of the buttons.

ALICE: I'm supposed to be impressed? Forget it, man! Any stiffhead can wire himself up. That's about all they can do.

CROWE: The boys in the radio van'll love you, sweetie. Come on! Do I look like a stiffhead to you?

ALICE: To be honest, man, yes!

CROWE: I take that as a compliment.

ALICE: To me, you look like a narc gone native.

CROWE: What better cover? You wear their clothes, speak their language...

ALICE: Take their drugs.

CROWE: Can't always fake it.

ALICE: That's how you got hooked.

CROWE: Who says I'm hooked? I can control it, man. That's what I'm trained to do.

The phone rings.

Leave it!

Phone keeps ringing.

ALICE: Let's see your arms.

CROWE: What? (*Impatiently picking up the phone.*) Yes? (*Listens.*) No. Quetzal Travel has ceased trading. As of now. (*Listens.*) The receiver. Yeah that's right, I'm the fucking receiver. Now fuck off! (*Slams down the phone.*) Fucking junkies!

ALICE: You may find this hard to get your head around, but this is a Travel Agency. The fact is, most people call to book flights.

CROWE: Yeah and I'm the Queen of fucking Sheba! Forget it, sweetie. We all buy the same ticket. We know what kind of flights we book with you!

ALICE: Your arms.

CROWE: The fact is! I am flying right here and now.

ALICE: Let's see them.

CROWE: Before your very eyes! What for?

ALICE: You know what for.

CROWE: Fuck you! My arms are my affair!

ALICE: I think that answers my question.

CROWE: Fuck you! All right. Why not? You want to see a work of art?

Rolls up his sleeve to reveal an arm pocked and scabbed with track-marks.

ALICE: Shit!

CROWE: Not a pretty sight, huh?

ALICE: How long you been fixing?

CROWE: You hear what I'm saying? A work of art –

ALICE: Junkie's tattoo. Well, you're the artist, man.

CROWE: You don't hear what I'm saying. This was done to me. Deliberately. With –

ALICE: (*Wearily.*) Yeah, yeah!

CROWE: Malice of forethought.

ALICE: You knew too much.

CROWE: Too right! I was all set to unmask him.

ALICE: "An order was given".

CROWE: By who? That's the question. Who gave the order?

ALICE: (*Sighs.*) Okay, Crowe. You tell me. Who? Who pushes the buttons?

CROWE abruptly rips off the battery pack and wiring, dumps it in the bin.

CROWE: Strictly off the record, okay? That was my big mistake, my report to Control... Filed a full report, target identification, the works. I was that close! Spelt it out. "Target: Iceman."

ALICE: (*Bemused.*) Iceman?

CROWE: You still don't get it, huh? I report to Control. I name names. I sign my own death warrant. (*Reliving the event.*) Next time I score, dealer invites me to sample the goods. Wants to see me jack up, right? Primes the spike, stands over me – make sure I don't try the old sleeve-trick. Man, I went out. Click.

ALICE: (*Shrugs.*) Dealers spiking narcs. Far as I'm concerned, you creeps're asking for it. But what's that got to do with the Iceman?

CROWE: Everything! He controls the dealer. He's the Man behind the Man...

ALICE: (*Slowly.*) Let's get this straight. The Iceman smells a narc and shoots you full of shit.

CROWE: How do you think he found out? Look at the timing. I'm telling you – it was an inside job. My cover was blown.

ALICE: (*Stunned.*) You trying to tell me... My source... The Iceman is a –

CROWE: He's the fucking narc! That's what I keep telling you. Our own man is pushing this shit. I need your help to bust a fucking narc!

Wanders aimlessly, reliving the event in present time.

Just as I'm going out, it clicks. It all clicks. It all goes... click.

Bumps into the desk.

Next thing I know, I'm walking around with a monkey on my back.

ALICE: Wow! (*Sits on the couch, stunned. Long pause.*) Why not just ice you and have done with it?

CROWE: That's not how he operates. It's not enough to kill me. He wants to control me. Absolutely. He wants me for his fucking zombie. That's where he fucked up. Only this time he fucked up good. I'm closing on him. Getting warm. Or is it cold? We are talking Ice, right? I can see him, yes, he's coming into focus... Ice sensitizes your intuition.

ALICE: Certainly wipes out all your other faculties.

CROWE: No, it's selective. Precision bombing. Takes out specific nodes... That's the idea. Turn us all into fucking machines, unless... Unless I get to him first. I need your help.

ALICE: To set a trap? "Entrapment." (*Sighs.*) Why me?

CROWE: Have to trust someone.

Sprawls beside her on the couch, almost succumbing to the onrush of the psychedelic truth-drug used to spike his coffee.

I need... a name.

ALICE: I thought you were the one who "named names".

CROWE: He uses many names. You know the need I name... (*Corrects himself, with an effort.*) Name I need.

ALICE: You've never met. Not face to face. How are you supposed to know who the hell you're after? And if I tell you, take you to the Man, what do you do then? Burst in, guns blazing?

CROWE registers that he is tripping. He jumps up, staring at her. He backs away to the desk, crashing into it. Tense pause.

Man, you look like shit! You want some more coffee? (*Makes to get coffee.*)

CROWE: (*Pointedly, with a hint of menace.*) I think I've drunk enough coffee for one night. Don't you?

ALICE: (*Stops, off his suspicious look.*) What?

CROWE: What if... What if he sent you?

ALICE: Who?

CROWE: The Iceman... sent you to... shut me down...

ALICE: Stiffheads! Try so hard to fit it all together, you can't see it when it's in your face.

CROWE: What if –

ALICE: What if I tell you he doesn't exist?

CROWE: (*Pause.*) Your source? (*Pause.*) You're saying...

ALICE: There is no source.

CROWE: (*Takes time to process the information.*) Then...
   There's no one behind you. This is your set-up.
   You're one of us. Another fucking narc!

ALICE: I'm afraid so. (*Pause.*)

CROWE: Well, fuck me!

   *Has a fit of giggles. ALICE laughs. CROWE freezes,
   staring at her.*

ALICE: (*As if telling a joke.*) Two coppers on acid, right?
   Both posing as Heads, but using their heightened
   awareness to suss each other out. So it's like, I turn to
   you and say: "Hey, man. You're a cop." And you say:
   "Well, fuck me! So are you." (*Laughs nervously.*)

CROWE: What the fuck is this?

ALICE: So I say to you: "We're tripped out of our skulls
   on illicit substances. We're breaking the law." And
   you say: "We are the law! So what we gonna do,
   arrest ourselves?"

CROWE: That story's being going the rounds since
   Operation Julie.

ALICE: "Better keep ourselves under surveillance."

CROWE: You're just giving me –

ALICE: Dose of your own medicine.

CROWE: What the – (*Reacts to a vivid hallucination,
   clutching at the chair for support.*) What did you put in
   the coffee?

ALICE: Thought you squirted it up your sleeve.

CROWE: (*Delves into his coat, pulling a gun.*) Freeze!

Aims the gun at her, making a supreme effort to resist the effects of the drug.

You're under arrest.

ALICE: (*Unimpressed.*) I don't have to say anything –

CROWE: You talk. Or you fucking die! Okay?

The door-bell rings. Both freeze. TV screen lights up: BUZZ, smiling into the security camera. CROWE nods.

ALICE: (*Speaks into intercom.*) Hi, Buzz. (*Presses button to release outer door.*)

CROWE: See what he's got for us, shall we? Just remember. Nobody wants to get hurt.

Pointedly slips the gun into his waistband, covering it with his shirt. BUZZ appears, holding a black attaché case. ALICE unlocks the cell-door to let him in. They act as if nothing has happened.

ALICE: How'd it go, Buzz?

BUZZ: Piece of cake.

CROWE: How was the pizza?

BUZZ: (*Glances quizzically at ALICE, who gives him the nod.*) Nice, man. Yeh! Piece of pizza! How you two getting on?

ALICE: House on fire.

CROWE: You got the gear?

BUZZ: Safe, man. The best.

CROWE: Source happy?

BUZZ: Happy, man. Happy? The Man over the moon! (*Setting the case on the desk.*) Let's take a closer look. Here! Cue music.

Music: with sampled Native American beats and ritual chants. Trippy club lighting. BUZZ opens the case with a flourish, going into his "routine". The case is empty. CROWE stares into it, his bewilderment turning to rage.

The best, man. Brujo the name and this here is my magic medicine bag... Mushrooms. Magic herb and root. Peyote. Datura. Belladonna. This one Yage, telepathic bark direct from the Amazon – (*CROWE grabs him by the throat.*) Hey!

CROWE: Okay, Buzz –

BUZZ: Brujo the name, man. Brujo!

Gives the word its guttural Spanish pronunciation: "Brucho", jabbing with his finger. CROWE releases his grip, gasping.

Brujo, man. Witch doctor. Medicine man.

CROWE: Cut it, man! The fucking case is empty.

ALICE: You mean the case is closed.

CROWE: I know what you're trying to lay on me.

CROWE grabs the case, turns it upside down, shaking it.

BUZZ: Hey, chill out, man. Now look what you've done!

Goes down on his knees, pretending to gather up the contents of the case.

Mucho dinaros!

ALICE joins BUZZ, pretending to help gather the contents.

CROWE: No... Nothing there... Empty...

BUZZ: (*Holding up an invisible lizard.*) Take a look at that, babes.

ALICE: What is it?

BUZZ: Lizard.

ALICE: Yes. It's a lizard. Why are the eyes sewn shut?

BUZZ: Old brujo trick. Train it to look within.

ALICE: (*Stares at invisible lizard.*) Stitch up its eyes?

BUZZ: Feed it to the Crow.

ALICE: That's so cruel.

BUZZ: We are cruel to the body. (*To CROWE.*) You are cruel to the spirit.

CROWE: You spiked the fucking coffee!

ALICE: You buys your ticket. You crosses over.

BUZZ: Cross-over, man. We crossing you over.

CROWE: Not me, man. I'm staying right here.

ALICE: (*To BUZZ.*) Tell him, senor, how he may cross over.

BUZZ: Gringo!

Takes out the map, handing it to CROWE.

CROWE: (*Staring at it.*) What's this?

ALICE: A map.

BUZZ: Codex, man.

CROWE: Tourist map... Guatemala...

BUZZ: Is a hidden map, Crow-man.

ALICE: The image is superimposed.

BUZZ: Have to see behind the surface. You see it? You crossed over.

ALICE: You're on the Other Side.

BUZZ: Inside. You see? Penetration.

ALICE: You're safe here, Crowe. They can't find you here.

BUZZ: We hidden, like the map inside the map.

CROWE: What time is it? How long have we been here?

BUZZ: No time, man. Time is dead. We always been here.

ALICE: It's safe to talk.

CROWE: And then?

BUZZ: Crow get to eat the lizard.

CROWE suddenly screws up the map, throwing it away.

CROWE: Fuck you! I know what's going down here.

BUZZ: Cut! (*Music stops.*)

CROWE: I see what you're trying to lay on me.

ALICE: He's not as far gone as we thought.

BUZZ: You saw it, man, admit it. You saw the lizard.

CROWE: I saw through it.

ALICE: (*To BUZZ.*) He did.

BUZZ: Then there's hope.

CROWE: Look! (*Holds up the empty case.*) Empty! Well?

BUZZ: (*Innocently.*) Oh, yeh! The Man says he can't deliver. Not tonight anyhow. Maybe tomorrow.

CROWE: Bull Shit! (*To ALICE.*) You slipped him the word, one of your codes, to pack his bags and get out. Get "Brujo" here to do a dummy run, keep me guessing. (*To BUZZ.*) What was the code? Pizza?

BUZZ: (*To ALICE.*) You better fill me in, babes.

CROWE: You sussed what I am and cancelled the deal.

BUZZ: What you are? What the fuck are you, man?

ALICE: Turns out we been doing business with a narc.

CROWE: With a C.

BUZZ: A "C", man? (*Pause. Slumps on the couch.*) Shit!

ALICE: No shit.

> *CROWE takes the opportunity to reassert his authority. He moves in on BUZZ, holding the bottle of "Truth".*

CROWE: No, but you and your girlfriend here are in deep shit. You think you can get away with an empty case and some stiffhead mind-fuck routine? You spiked my coffee.

BUZZ: True, man.

CROWE: (*Showing BUZZ the bottle.*) What is it? Acid?

BUZZ: The Truth, man. LSD cut with sodium pentothal. Is a truth drug. As secretly tested by the CIA.

CROWE: You all make the same mistake. Anything you care to dump on me, I can take it.

BUZZ: You can't bust us for pushing the truth, man.

CROWE: Spiking a police officer? Take it from me, Buzz, you better have a fucking good brief.

> *Holds up bottle.*

Acid...

> *Holds up the bag of crystals.*

Ice...

BUZZ: (*To ALICE, accusingly.*) Fuck, man! The samples.

ALICE: (*Dryly.*) What's left of them.

BUZZ: He can get us for possession.

CROWE: (*Indicates the other drugs on the desk.*) Hashish... And what have we here? (*Holds up the syringe and the bag of brown powder.*) Our old friend Henry the Horse...

BUZZ: Nothing to do with us, man. I say you planted it. Our word against yours.

CROWE: Not to mention a thirty kilo Ice deal.

BUZZ: Where, man? Where's your evidence?

CROWE: So? You smell a rat and try to welch... (*Triumphantly, pointing at ALICE.*) But not before the Ice Queen leaves her fingerprints all over the marked bank-notes – (*Seized by a sudden panic.*) Where is it?

BUZZ: Where's what, man?

CROWE: The money. My one twenty fucking K! You didn't score. Where the fuck is it?

BUZZ: Oh, shit! I must've left it in the pizza parlour.

ALICE: Fuck the money, man. We're way past that.

CROWE: Yeah, fuck the money! And fuck you! You guys are well and truly fucked, believe me! This place is being watched from all angles, entries, exits. Your friend Brujo was followed to the pizzeria. The case has been retrieved. They'll be matching your prints. Our entire conversation has been transmitted to a radio-van... (*ALICE laughs.*) What's so funny? When you're doing time...

ALICE: You've looped back into an old track.

CROWE: Scum like you, pushing this shit in kiddies' playgrounds.

ALICE: No way, Crowe! No way back. The old tracks are wiped. You see, Buzz, while you were out eating your pizza, your man Crowe has been revealing – well, not quite all, but – I tell you, Buzz – quite a revelation!

BUZZ: What exactly did my man reveal?

ALICE: Well, for starters, seems your man is on some kind of suicide mission to bust the entire fucking drug squad. According to your man, and I quote: "We are the drug problem".

CROWE: Too right, man! And here's my living proof – two narcs caught red-handed –

BUZZ: Narcs? (*To ALICE.*) He knows? (*She nods.*) You weren't supposed to tell him –

ALICE: He worked it out for himself –

BUZZ: Not until we go live in the studio –

ALICE: I know, Buzz. This entire evening hasn't gone exactly to plan. For fuck's sake, improvise!

BUZZ: So. We're the law. Well... That's a relief.

Sits behind the desk, relaxing.

CROWE: It won't do you any good.

BUZZ: Come on, man, you can't go round busting police officers.

CROWE: That's exactly what I intend to do.

BUZZ: (*To ALICE.*) He's bluffing, babes.

ALICE: Yes. You see, Crowe, this here's the bait. (*Indicates the drugs on the desk.*) The set-up. All this can be explained in the context of your case.

CROWE: *My* case?

BUZZ: Better watch your back, man. If we the law, looks like we here to bust you.

CROWE: I was expecting that. You think you fool me with your truth drugs and... find-muck routines? The old mirror trick!

BUZZ: You the man in the mirror, man. Crow-man look in the mirror, see it all back to front.

CROWE: And where's *your* evidence? Jesus! In all my years in the force, I never saw such a shabby operation. You bust me? You guys couldn't run-in a fucking glue sniffer.

BUZZ: (*Laughs, breaking the tension.*) Hey, let's not fight among ourselves. We all in the same game, no? Undercovers Anonymous. We can hold a narcs' convention. What do you say? Smoke some crack, watch an adult video. (*Points at the TV screen. CROWE reacts.*) It's cool, man. Look! (*Holds up his finger.*) I can't shoot you with this. Or can I? (*"firing" at the screen.*) Bang!

TV screen lights up: the FACE, a shifting mosaic of flesh-tones, as before. Music. BUZZ raps.

Welcome to the Twilight Zone
With a nark in the dark you are never alone
Welcome to the cutting-room floor.
Check it out.

Ambient music. BUZZ observes CROWE, who stares at the screen in disbelief.

No, man. That's not the coffee.

ALICE: The face has been processed to protect the innocent.

CONTROL: *Ice Man?*

FACE: *Ice, Snow, Rain, you name it – the Man can deliver, bulk!*

CONTROL: *You say he's one of ours.*

CROWE: What the fuck!

CONTROL: *Can you be more explicit?*

FACE: *Hard to put your finger on.*

CROWE: How the fuck d'you get hold of this?

FACE: *Patterns... Dealer gets busted; Iceman moves in to take his place.*

ALICE: Your report to Control. Remember?

FACE: *The coke dries up; we all start smoking crack.*

ALICE: That's you on screen, reporting, right?

FACE: *We have to move quickly. He's starting to suspect. Like most junkies, he's totally paranoid. He's also acquired a taste for his own Ice. I tell you, man, he is totally... fucked!*

CROWE: So what does that prove? I told you I reported –

ALICE: Proves you told the truth.

CONTROL: *We can't proceed without an identification.*

ALICE: And that we have access to your Control.

CONTROL: *Target identification.*

CROWE: And that Control blew my cover!

CONTROL: *We need a name.*

ALICE: Listen!

FACE: (*The voice distorting.*) *Some asshole goes by the name of... Crowe... Crowe... Crowe... Crowe...*

BUZZ: Freeze!

"Fires" at the screen: freezing the frame. CROWE turns slowly away from the frozen, scrambled face, in shock.

ALICE: It fits, Crowe. The Face fits. Like all good cover stories, yours was a version of the truth. You were an agent who became addicted in the course of duty. Like you said: you can't always shoot it up your sleeve. One morning Crowe wakes up with a bad habit. If he had any sense, he'd turn himself in for detox – but no. Maybe he thought he could beat it. "Yeh, man, I can kick any time." Only the time is never now, right? So while he's waiting to kick, he starts to deal some on the side, like the Man says, enough to support his habit.

CROWE wanders aimlessly, severely disorientated.

Eh, Crowe? The cop with a habit to feed. His own deep-cover – taking him over, turning him into Crowe the addict. But Crowe the cop hangs on in there, determined to crack his case. The man with two brains – the cop and the addict – both fighting for control. Before he knows it, he's narking on himself... I tell you, man, our shrinks've had a field-day with you. They authorised the truth-drug.

CROWE: They fucked with the tape! Dubbed my name!

ALICE: How many times, Crowe! There is no conspiracy. You named yourself!

CROWE: They sent you to... shut me down... You're here to... take me out.

ALICE: No. We're here to get you out in one piece.

CROWE: Going to arrest me for my own good?

ALICE: We're going to guide you through –

CROWE: (*Cackles.*) Alice through the looking-glass! They really got their rocks off with you, eh?

ALICE: Crowe, you fuckwit! I'm your only hope –

BUZZ: Cut it, babes. We got what we need. Going live to the studio. Lights. Camera. Action!

BUZZ points at the screen, which lights up with an image of the room as seen, live, through the hidden camera. CROWE stares at it, resisting what he sees.

CROWE: I know the routine. All done with mirrors...
That's how it's done... all... done... with... what the – ?!

Slowly moves in on the glass bird, picks it up, staring into the lens. His image fills the screen.

You're recording this?

ALICE: Your confession.

CROWE: You've got it all on tape?

BUZZ: Safe, man. You're a star.

CROWE: Cut!

Unplugs the lead. The screen goes blank. Music cuts out.

Pretty good. Pretty neat. Only... One thing you seem to forget...

Retrieves his tangled wiring from the bin.

I've got my own recordings. I think you'll find my recordings say something quite different.

ALICE: Your recording only exists in stiffhead reality.

BUZZ: True, Crow-man. No one receiving.

CROWE: You want me to call in my back-up?

ALICE: You have no back-up, man.

BUZZ: Your back-up fade away, melt into the night.

CROWE: I only have to give the word...

BUZZ: Give it. The word, man. Give the word.

CROWE: Fuck you! You're both under arrest.

BUZZ: (*Laughs.*) Oh, yeh, man? Let's see your warrant.

CROWE: (*Pulling out his gun.*) Here's my fucking warrant! Okay? All the warrant I need. I came here to make an arrest. (*Grabs ALICE, pressing the gun to her head. To BUZZ.*) Now. You. Are going to go back through that wall and fetch my case, with the cash, and bring it right back here, or your girlfriend's brains get to feed the fucking Rain God! (*Indicates the Aztec calendar.*)

BUZZ: No sweat, man. "Through the wall. Get the cash." Done. (*Disappears through the wall.*)

ALICE: Take that thing away from my head. You're not on TV now, you know.

CROWE steps back, covering her, still struggling to process the information.

CROWE: So... We all share the same Control... It all... connects... This room connects to other rooms... Where more of your goons are watching.

ALICE: And listening.

CROWE: No more. (*Shows her the unplugged glass-work.*) You know what they feed on? Images! And now we've cut-off the supply.

ALICE: It's all in the can. We've got more than enough.

CROWE: So... The recordings are made elsewhere. Yes... You got me... (*Pause.*) But I got you... Babes.

Circles her with controlled menace.

And if what you say is true, you're all I've got. And nothing to lose.

ALICE: We're all on the same side, Crowe. I was assigned to rescue an agent who'd become addicted in the field. Missing in action. You're not the first, believe me.

CROWE: You think being a cop makes you immune? You're the one under arrest! You're the... Jesus!

Aims the gun at her, making a last-ditch attempt to resist the effects of the drug.

Could take you out... Just like that...

ALICE: You could. But you won't. You know why? Because only I can deal with your hidden agenda. You came here looking for the Iceman, but deep down, deep, deep under deep-cover, you knew what you were walking into. You came to confess, to turn yourself in.

CROWE: I came here to... make... an arrest...

ALICE: A definitive arrest. And I'm here to help you make it. You see, Crowe? You're not just the sum of your covers. Deep down under the Iceman, there's a good copper, almost dead from frostbite. That's who we have to save.

CROWE: (*Lowers the gun, laughing.*) What is this? The Gentle Touch? Bust me on Ecstasy?

ALICE: We're here to bring in the agent, save him from the Iceman.

Under the influence of the truth-drug, CROWE becomes absorbed in trying to crack his own case.

CROWE: They're no longer separate entities. They've spliced the codes. You can't see where one ends and the other begins... You see how it works, how it fits together? Mathematical, like a Moroccan rip-off. The narc and the Iceman, each programmed to take out the other.

ALICE: No-one programmed you. You programmed yourself, to cover your own tracks.

CROWE: Oh, man, that's so beautiful. A Mandelbrod Set, with the narc and the Iceman as constant variables.

ALICE: But they can't exist in the same space and time.

CROWE: That's the problem.

ALICE: What if they do? What happens when their worlds collide?

CROWE: But they can't. They mustn't.

ALICE: But they do.

CROWE: But ... (*Struggling to resolve the paradox.*) Iceman...
I came here to... arrest the... Iceman... I am the Iceman...
(*It clicks.*) I'm under arrest. (*Pause.*) Well, fuck me rigid
with a twelve-inch...

*He has a fit of hysterical laughter, turning to cries of pain
as he collapses on the couch, shaken by jolts and spasms.
ALICE sits beside him, comforting him. He no longer has
the strength to resist.*

ALICE: Stay with it, Crowe. It'll pass. I'm here, and
Buzz too, when you need him. We'll get you out.

CROWE: And fuck you! Fuck you!

He gasps and groans, remembering.

I did. Oh Jesus. I did.

ALICE: Yes. You did. *We* did.

CROWE: The Welsh farmhouse. Girl with the shaved
head.

ALICE: Not that I've got old scores to settle. As I recall,
it was quite a good fuck.

CROWE: Oh Jesus.

He clings to her like a scared child. She holds him.

ALICE: When I took this assignment, believe me I
didn't know it was going to be you. Then when I
marked you at Speedy Kate's – I knew right away
– and yes, that gave me the edge – but it really
was nothing personal – just doing my job – but I
don't have to tell you that – you more than
anyone – how the job takes over your life...

CROWE: They're using you. Like they used me...

ALICE: Of course we get used. People want war on
drugs. Can you blame them? They want to know

their kids're safe to walk the streets at night. They don't want to know the sordid details.

CROWE: Take out take over...

ALICE: Yes, you and me, Crowe... We know the only way to stop the pushers is to become like them. No. Not "like". We become them. In no man's land... If our cover gets blown we're dead and if it's too good we're busted. We can't win. Is it any wonder we're so paranoid?

CROWE: It's all true... It's happening. Here...

The wall opens. BUZZ returns with the case, to find CROWE, shivering, in ALICE's arms.

BUZZ: Broken-wing John Crow. (*To CROWE.*) Got to hand it you, man. You held up better than we predicted.

ALICE: Buzz is a detox expert. You couldn't be in safer hands. You see? Your report to Control was a cry for help.

BUZZ: Or a severe case of brain damage.

ALICE: (*To BUZZ.*) He turned himself in. That in itself speaks in his favour.

CROWE: Favour?

BUZZ: Defence, man.

CROWE: I'm on trial. Already?

ALICE: There has to be some procedure... Don't worry. We all want this kept under wraps.

CROWE: Yeh! *They'll* take care of the cover-up.

ALICE: Your case will be dealt with internally.

CROWE: Internally! (*Howls with laughter.*)

BUZZ: You got it, bro'. Detox. Go thaw you out. Help you kick the habit –

CROWE: (*Jerks upright, in a spasm of inane giggles.*) You think that'll stop me? I don't need Crowe. I'm done with Crowe... (*Raps like one possessed.*) Crowe got clever. Crowe got insight. Crowe got too close and got a bad case of frostbite... Crowe got smart Crowe thought he could trick me. Crowe took the cure but he still couldn't kick me...

Convulses.

ALICE: (*To BUZZ.*) For fuck's sake! How much did you give him?

CROWE: So fuck much. Oh, God!

BUZZ: I know, man. I been there.

Primes a syringe, drawing a measured dose from one of the phials.

ALICE: It's okay, Crowe, stay with it. You're not going to die.

CROWE: I'm done with Crowe. You flush me out, I just slip on another skin. Yours for instance. Easy! You be so easy – you're – just like... me... Who? Me? Your Other Half... Face in your mirror...

ALICE: He's all yours, Buzz. Put him out of his misery.

BUZZ: No sweat, man.

Gently taking CROWE's arm, injects him. CROWE makes a last feeble attempt to resist.

CROWE: Ouch! Now they're shooting me up! Again! What is it this time? Methadone? Turn me into a methadone junkie! Worst of all possible worlds! Highly addictive and you don't even get high.

BUZZ: Chlorpromazine. Fifty milligrams. As prescribed by Dr Albert Hoffmann, the father of LSD. Guaranteed to bring you down fast. And a shot of librium to get you through the night.

CROWE: I know how to handle a fucking comedown. I don't need your fucking cure.

ALICE: You will, Crowe, believe me. I guarantee you've never had a comedown like this.

CROWE: (*Speaking with difficulty.*) Frozen turkey? So close... Ice Queen... One kiss... Freeze!

ALICE: It's all right, Crowe. I'm right here with you.

CROWE: I want this witness... I want... I want this... on the record... that... that...

ALICE: Hang on in there.

CROWE: That... this...

ALICE: I'll see you through.

CROWE: This... was... done... to... me...

Passes out.

BUZZ: He's gone, babes.

ALICE: You call an ambulance?

BUZZ: On its way. (*Pause.*) Don't look good, girl. We'll salvage what we can, but... (*Shrugs.*) Never get them back in one piece.

ALICE: Your cure, man. Worse than the disease! What a fucking waste!

BUZZ: All in a good cause.

ALICE: Not the way he received it. His recordings say we shut him down, by order of the Iceman.

BUZZ: Speedfreaks, man! Believe the weirdest things.

ALICE: Can you blame him? We spike his coffee, rip him off something rotten, shoot him full of shit –

BUZZ: Remember what I told you.

ALICE: Yeh. (*To CROWE.*) Buzz's right. Can't afford to get personal. You're just a john, another john, another fucking john. Nothing personal, John.

BUZZ: Could be me, babes. Could be you.

ALICE: My Other Half. For what, Buzz? A war we can't win. When the only way to fight it is to turn into the enemy –

BUZZ: Don't babes. That's Crow-talk. Look what talk like that done to Crow!

Clicks his fingers to his mournful rap.

Welcome to the Killing Floor
Don't ask me what we fightin' for
Welcome to the Twilight Zone.

Pause. She does not respond.

But if you don't stop the Bully Boys
Kickin' down your neighbour door
Soon they be kickin' down your own.

Breaks off from the rap.

Till one day The Man come for me and you.

ALICE: You got it. So where does that leave us?

BUZZ: With a case full of frozen assets. Enough to keep this show on the road.

Opens the case, brandishing a wad of banknotes, trying to cheer her up.

What do you say, we take the money and run? Split to Guatemala, check out the quetzal bird.

No response. He closes the case.

Don't ask me, babes. I'm only a technician. Just doing my job.

Opens the wall, disappearing through it, leaving her alone with CROWE. ALICE stares at the supine CROWE, twitching and jerking in his sleep. The phone rings. She answers it.

ALICE: Quetzal Travel... (*Listens.*) There must be some mistake... We didn't order pizza...

Hangs up, shaken. TV screen suddenly flashes on: the FACE, interviewed by CONTROL, as before, with the volume cranked up.

CONTROL: Ice Man?

Music kicks in, loud and menacing.

FACE: Ice, Snow, Rain, you name it – the Man can deliver, bulk!

CONTROL: You say he's one of ours. (*Pause.*) Can you be more explicit?

FACE: Hard to put your finger on. Patterns...

ALICE: (*Calling out.*) Buzz?

FACE: Dealer gets busted; Iceman moves in to take his place.

ALICE: (*Shouting.*) Buzz!

FACE: The coke dries up; we all start smoking crack.

ALICE: Turn that fucking thing off!

Blackout. The on-screen image persists: a shifting mosaic of flesh-tones. The sinister music builds to a crescendo. Screen blacks out.

The End

THE FALSE HAIRPIECE

CHARACTERS

DA

MA

CLAUDETTE

CHARLES

JAKE

The action takes place on the Crow Farm somewhere in Hampshire.

The False Hairpiece was first produced by Proteus, directed by Chris Baldwin, with the following cast:

DA, Stuart Mullen

MA, Juliet Alderdice

CLAUDETTE, Odette Cohen

CHARLES, Kevin Hosier

JAKE, Stuart Mullen

Designed by Petrina Boddington.

Music by Paul Barker.

ACT ONE

Scene 1

Elegiac music. Dim blue light on DA slumped in a wheelchair, a once robust man stricken with motor neuron disease. He's in his dressing-gown, his legs covered by a blanket. He wears glasses with thick lenses that magnify his eyes, his face lit by the phosphorescent glow of a computer screen. The screen and an amplifier are attached to the wheelchair, parts of a voice-synthesizer controlled by a panel on one of the arms. He stares at the screen, immobile. Only his hand twitches at the panel to activate the voice-synthesizer. The amplifier relays his echoing machine-voice.

DA: And the Lord said unto her...

Two nations are in thy womb...

And two manner of people shall be separated from thy bowels...

And the one people shall be stronger than the other people...

And the elder shall serve the younger...

Genesis... twenty-five... twenty-three..

Light fades to black. Music fades to lights up on: The kitchen of an old farmhouse. The set is heightened with distorted perspectives, and encased in a womb-like tent. Upstage, right to left: a stove; pots and pans and a shotgun hung on pegs; steps leading up to a cupboard in the wall. Downstage right: door to the scullery. Up left: door to the hall, front door and other rooms. A sturdy old wooden table and chairs, and a solitary armchair covered with a dust-sheet. DA is in his wheelchair. MA ushers in CLAUDETTE, a young professional woman in a smart business-suit, clutching her briefcase. MA wears slacks and an old sweater. She turns DA to face CLAUDETTE, speaking in the cheery sing-song voice generally reserved for children and invalids.

MA: Here we are...

CLAUDETTE: (*Clears her throat.*) Mr Crow, my name's Claudette Meier... (*He doesn't react. To MA.*) Is he... Can he...

MA: He knows you're there. (*Fusses over DA, tucking in his blanket.*) The Da's eyes aren't what they used to be, but he doesn't miss a trick, do you Da? He got our son to call your office.

CLAUDETTE: Ah, yes... Charles?

MA: Behind my back. He knows I don't approve. All this fuss... (*To DA.*) Say hello to the lady. (*DA stares at the screen, his hand twitching at the control panel. To CLAUDETTE.*) It's a shame! Still, isn't it marvellous what they can do with machines these days?

DA: (*Activates the voice-synthesizer, "speaking" in his machine-voice.*) Matheson...

MA: (*To CLAUDETTE.*) He'd already recorded his message for Mr –

DA: Matheson...

MA: (*To DA, patiently.*) Mr Matheson can't come today. This is Miss –

DA: Matheson...

MA: Meier. Miss Meier.

CLAUDETTE: Claudette. (*Unpacking her briefcase on the table.*) I er... I believe... Mr Matheson did in fact attend to you in person on the er... (*Consults her notes.*) seventeenth? And before that on the fifth. This is the er... third change this month.

MA: (*To DA.*) What did I tell you? He's sick and tired of fussing over your blinking will. Miss Meier's his assistant, aren't you dear?

CLAUDETTE: Not exactly. That is, I am what's called an assistant solicitor. But that doesn't mean I'm not... I mean, I am qualified. As a matter of fact I specialised in probate law. And of course I have been fully briefed by Mr Matheson.

DA: I want it sorted out before I go...

MA: (*To CLAUDETTE.*) Hark at him! (*To DA.*) You're not going anywhere. You're going to get better.

DA: Before I kick the bucket...

MA: You're not going to die. (*To CLAUDETTE.*) He's not. Is he? (*Fiercely.*) He's not going to die.

CLAUDETTE: I er... I was given to understand that Mr Crow simply wishes to put his affairs in order.

MA: (*Sighs.*) He frets you see. Now he can't work – it all happened so suddenly. I don't know where we'd've been without Charles. He gave up medicine to take over the farm. Well, the management. Muggins here still does the donkey-work – so now he just sits there, recording his little messages.

DA: Don't let her switch me off...

MA: You – silly! No-one's going to switch you off. (*To CLAUDETTE.*) The things they say!

DA: Old cock can't even crow...

MA: Da! What will Claudette think?

DA: Old Dick he went a-rooting...

MA: She'll think we're always arguing. (*CLAUDETTE is leafing through her papers, doing her best not to get involved.*) So let's all make a big effort to be nice. Shall we?

CLAUDETTE: We did obtain permission from the Public Health Department for Mr Crow's request to be buried in the family plot, in the field behind the er... (*Consults her papers.*) cowshed. Provided the grave is located not less than thirty yards from the er... livestock. (*Clears her throat.*) Now as it stands, Mr Crow bequeaths the farm to his son Charles –

DA: Jake...

CLAUDETTE: (*Consults the will.*) With provision for a trust fund for his elder son –

DA: Jake... The farm goes to Jake...

Stunned silence. MA laughs nervously.

MA: You can't do that!

DA: I will...

MA: The Farm?

DA: To Jake...

MA: What about Charles? You've already willed him the farm.

DA: You talked me into it...

MA: I just tried to talk some sense into you! (*Appealing to CLAUDETTE.*) There's nothing in law says I can't influence his decision. Is there?

CLAUDETTE: Well, no... It's entirely reasonable that the testator should wish to consult with his spouse and dependents –

MA: You see! Even Miss Meier says you're being unreasonable.

CLAUDETTE: Provided no undue pressure is brought to bear.

MA: Charles is the manager. He's been running it ever since poor Da –

DA: Jake gets the deeds...

MA: And where does that leave Charles?

DA: He'll manage... Haha...

MA: Da! Please. You mustn't do this. It's not fair on either of them. (*To CLAUDETTE.*) Poor Jake has enough problems...

DA: This is my last will and testament...

MA: You're doing this to punish me. (*To CLAUDETTE.*) Please! Try to talk some sense into him.

CLAUDETTE: It's hardly my place to offer an opinion.

MA: (*To DA.*) You see? Claudette thinks you're trying to upset me.

CLAUDETTE: However, I would certainly be failing in my duty if I failed to point out to my client that the very existence of such contradictory instructions could be construed as admitting grounds for contesting the will.

MA: (*To DA.*) I hope you're listening to this.

DA: So let's keep it country simple... Haha... I leave the lot to Jake... And to hell with you and Charlie...

MA: Da! And after all we've done for you.

DA: Always... creeping... round me...

MA: We just want you to get better.

DA: All ways so bloody... unn... ttt... uuu... ooo... uuu...

MA: (*Alarmed.*) Da! Da... What is it? What have you done now?

DA: I'm all right... It's this bloody voice box...

MA: (*To CLAUDETTE.*) It upsets me to see him in this state.

DA: Unctuous... Unctuous...

MA: The doctor says he mustn't get excited.

DA: Damn the doctor... They all want a piece of me...

MA: We don't want your blinking money – you're the one lies awake all night fussing over it. (*To CLAUDETTE.*) It's my own fault. I always let him take care of things like that. Charles was shocked when he found out I didn't have my own bank-account, didn't even know what bills need paying. (*Cries.*) He can be so hurtful sometimes... He doesn't mean it. (*Blows her nose.*) It's been hard.

CLAUDETTE: It can't have been easy.

MA: You can't imagine.

DA: Jake... Where's Jake...

MA: (*Beat.*) Where do you think he is?

DA: I want to talk to him...

MA: I told you – he doesn't want to talk to you. You know how sensitive he is. This whole business has upset him.

DA: Jake was here... He came to me...

MA: (*Startled.*) What? When?

DA: Haha... Last night...

MA: (*To CLAUDETTE.*) It's impossible. Jake couldn't have been here... I mean, he wouldn't... He gets confused, you see – Da. He imagines things. He's in no state to know what's what...

CLAUDETTE: Er... Mrs Crow... (*Taking MA aside.*) You put me in a very difficult position. If you're suggesting that your husband is not competent to revise his will –

DA: Genesis twenty-five twenty-three... And the Lord said unto her...

MA: (*Hushed voice.*) Well, what do *you* think? Just listen to him!

DA: I... Isaac Crow... being of sound mind...

CLAUDETTE: (*To MA.*) I'm not qualified to express an opinion.

DA: Do hereby bequeath my entire estate to my son...

CLAUDETTE: But if you're saying you intend to contest the will –

DA: Jake... Where's Jake...

MA: You want Jake? Alright, alright, I'll try and get him to come and talk to you. But I warn you, you won't like what he's got to say.

MA bustles off, leaving CLAUDETTE alone with DA.

DA: Haha... Love me to death... She's put up with a lot from me...

CLAUDETTE: I can imagine!

Awkward pause. She moves tentatively towards him, places a hand on his shoulder. He doesn't respond.

I... I'm sorry... It must be...

DA: Now she's got me where she wants me... Turn me into one of her boys...

CLAUDETTE moves away. DA's "voice" booms out, crackling with static, as if through a short-wave radio.

Listen... I'm a dead man...

CLAUDETTE stops, freezes.

I see my own flesh and blood... kith and kindred... Sins of the fathers... Brother against brother... The Dick and the Da and the thing best unsaid...

Listen... The Fall and... Nightmare Death...
Britain's Last Good Man... Honest and True...
Listen... Listen to this dead man talking...
Renew all... new life... new blood... Jake...
Jake knows... Heal... the rift...
Heal... the sick earth... mad meat machine...

*DA's "voice" resumes its normal volume. MA bustles back
in, giving CLAUDETTE a long-suffering look.*

Heal... the mad cow...

MA: What he on about now?

DA: Jake...

MA: (*Calling.*) Jake! Your Da wants a word with you.

*Enter "JAKE", a scruffy man in his thirties with long
matted hair, wearing the ragged clothes of a traveller. He
is evidently uncomfortable in their presence, a reluctant
accessory to whatever's going on between DA and MA.*

Jake, this is Miss Meier, the solicitor. (*To CLAUDETTE.*)
Jake, our eldest. By a couple of minutes. They're twins,
him and Charles.

"JAKE": Hello, Da. How's tricks?

DA: Jake... I want you to have...

"JAKE": The farm. Yes, Ma said... Well, thanks, Da –
but no thanks. I mean no hard feelings and nice of
you to think of me and all that, but I've always been
a bit of a black sheep and – well, not to put too fine a
point on it, you know I'm not to be trusted with
money. Let's face it, Da, I have enough trouble
without trying to run a farm. I wouldn't know one
end of a cow from the udder.

DA: Haha...

"JAKE": The cows are dead. I know, Da. Even I know
about the cows. We're talking turkey. Factory farming.

You know me, Da – haven't the stomach for it. Not that
I'm fanatic like some of my vegan chums, but I won't
eat anything that hasn't had some sort of a life, you
know – sun and fresh air, frisk in a field, one good f –

MA: (*Sharply.*) You watch your language, young man!

"JAKE": Frolic.

DA: Do what thou wilt...

"JAKE": Free the turkeys? Then what?

DA: Whatever it takes... Renew all... Jake...

"JAKE": And what happens to poor old Ma? Eh? No,
Da, take my advice. Leave the farm to Charlie. He'll
see I'm taken care of.

DA: Where's Charlie...

"JAKE": Dunno... Milking the cows? Torturing the
turkeys.

DA: You'll see them all right Jake...

"JAKE": I won't, Da, believe me. I'll see 'em all wrong.
I won't mean to but I will.

DA: I will it... to you...

"JAKE": But why, Da? Why? When I don't even want it.

DA: That's why... Claudette...

CLAUDETTE: Sir?

DA: How do we do this...

CLAUDETTE: Well, er... In normal circumstances, we'd
simply append a codicil...

DA: Do it...

CLAUDETTE: However, given the er... contentious
nature of the er... bequest... I'd like to talk it through
with Mr Matheson before drafting the –

DA: Now...

CLAUDETTE: Er... As you wish. Do you have witnesses?

DA: (*Beat.*) Jake... Jake's my witness...

CLAUDETTE: Ah, yes, but no, he can't, you see, I mean in law, he can't witness a will to which he is the sole beneficiary.

DA: Ma...

MA: I'm not witnessing anything.

DA: Charlie...

CLAUDETTE: Under the circumstances, I must advise that your two witnesses should not be family members.

MA: I did tell you. You weren't listening. He never listens to what I say.

CLAUDETTE: Do you have... servants or –

MA: (*Laughs.*) Who do you think we are? You hear that, Da? Servants! You see where it gets you, all this fussing over the farm. Claudette thinks you've got a crock of gold squirrelled away somewhere.

CLAUDETTE: Farm-workers?

MA: I told you – just me and Charles – unless you want to run the Da down to the village...

CLAUDETTE: I think it might be best if I come back another day.

DA: No... Claudette... Don't go...

CLAUDETTE: (*Touches him on the shoulder.*) I could come tomorrow.

DA: Tomorrow... I'm a dead man...

MA: Hark at him! He's been saying that for weeks. (*Ushering CLAUDETTE out.*) I'm sorry to put you to so much bother. (*Off her look.*) I did tell him, about the witnesses.

CLAUDETTE: (*Hesitates.*) If you want, I could arrange for two witnesses –

DA: Too late...

MA: Charles'll take care of it. I'll get him to phone your office tomorrow.

CLAUDETTE: Goodbye, Mr Crow.

MA escorts her off and out, leaving DA alone with "JAKE".

DA: Jake... Jake...

"JAKE": (*Close to tears.*) Da?

DA: Here... Y'old bugger... If you won't have the farm... You zul have your old Da's blessing... Here... Jake.

"JAKE" can take no more. He tears off the long-haired wig, exposing the cropped brother, CHARLES.

Charlie...

CHARLES breaks down, resuming his own distinct voice.

CHARLES: Oh, Da... Da... I'm so sorry... It was Ma... I... I... I'm sorry, Da... Sorry... Sorry, Da... So sorry...

DA: Haha... You want to hear your old... Da's... curse... Hear your old... Da curse you with his dying...

MA reappears, sizing up the situation at a glance. She briskly switches off DA's voice-box.

MA: That's enough of that.

CHARLES: (*Horrified.*) Ma! We can't just switch him off.

MA: It's for his own good. He thank us when he's better.

CHARLES: He isn't going to get better. Ma! He's dying in there.

MA: Don't talk such nonsense.

CHARLES: He cursed me, Ma.

MA: He didn't mean it.

CHARLES: His dying breath.

MA: Charles! Nobody's going to D... I... E... We're going to make you get better, aren't we Da?

DA, slumped in his wheelchair, does not respond. She picks up the discarded wig. Brightly:

Let's all be friends. Go on, Da. Tell Charles you didn't mean it. (*DA does not respond. To CHARLES.*) Da says he didn't mean it... (*CHARLES stares at her, aghast.*) I don't know. What a fuss! Come on, Da... Dinner-time!

MA wheels DA off, leaving CHARLES alone.

CHARLES: I'm sorry... Da...

Lights fade. In the darkness: sacred music. DA's machine-voice crackling with static.

DA: Name of the Da... Name of the son... Jake...
Art not thy brother's keeper...
Thy own flesh... and spirit... kith and kin... dread...
Hereditary disorder...
Genesis twenty-five twenty-three...
Heal... Two nations in thy womb, Ma...
Smooth man... Hairy man...
Man of the open spaces...
Heal them... Forgive them... Jake... Forgive...

Music fades.

Scene 2

The kitchen. Two weeks later. Late night. Lights up on MA, wearing Da's old dressing gown, sat on the steps to the now padlocked cupboard, her shopping trolley parked beside her. She's scribbling in a large bound book.

CHARLES: (*Off.*) Ma?

MA furtively closes the book. Enter CHARLES, half-dressed.

I saw the light on. Are you all right?

MA: Oh don't worry about me. I haven't had a good night's rest since your poor Da... He wasn't an easy man, your Da, especially those last days.

CHARLES: I know, Ma... We all know what you had to put up with.

MA: Oh you get to know their little ways.

CHARLES: He could be a cantankerous old bugger at the best of times.

MA: The worst was to see him like that. Oh, Charles it was so cruel! He was such an active man, always a mind of his own – and to find himself reduced to... I even had to wipe his bottom.

CHARLES: Try not to think about it, Ma.

MA: He hated it!

CHARLES: You'll only upset yourself.

MA: That's why he said those horrid hurtful things.

CHARLES: I'm sure he didn't mean them.

MA: It's an awful thing to say, but – in a way it was a relief.

CHARLES: I know.

MA: But I do miss not having him around. I only wish I could say he was in a happier place... (*Gripping him in panic.*) Oh, Charles, I do hope we've done the right thing.

CHARLES: So do I, believe me, but I'm not so sure about that –

MA: Well what were we supposed to do? I dread to think what would happen if Jake got his hands on it. (*Off his look.*) Oh I know you always jump to his defence – I'm glad you do, we always brought you up to look out for each other – but you know what he's like. He's so trusting your brother, easily led. Before we knew it, the whole place'd be crawling with tinkers.

CHARLES: Not tinkers, Ma. Travellers. (*Broods.*) What's done is done. I'm going to have to live with having cheated my own brother –

MA: Don't be silly! You were protecting his interests. It wouldn't have been fair on Jake. If he were here now I'm sure he'd say it's all for the best.

CHARLES: He would! Yes, if we'd talked to him, explained the situation – he'd have said yes, why not? He never wanted the farm. But he wasn't here to ask, and now we'll never be able to tell him.

MA: You'll see he's looked after.

CHARLES: And for what? The farm? It's hardly worth fighting over.

MA: If your poor Da could hear you now!

CHARLES: But it's true. We've lost the beef herd, the turkeys barely pay their way, if it wasn't for the set-aside we'd've gone under years ago.

MA: You'll find a way, if anyone can. I know I can count on you. (*Hugs him.*) Charles... I don't know where I'd be without you.

CHARLES: (*Breaks free.*) I wish I'd never let you talk me into wearing that stupid wig. Didn't do any good. Da saw right through me. He cursed me.

MA: He didn't know what he was saying. He thought Jake was here. No, you were very good. Even I almost believed you, especially the corny jokes. (*Chuckles.*) One end of the cow from the udder – that could have one of been Jake's.

CHARLES: It *was* one of Jake's. I stole all his best lines. You made me go through that whole charade –

MA: Don't blame me! If you hadn't gone and phoned Matheson –

CHARLES: I told you – the old man kept on at me.

MA: I do wish you'd told me before you went and –

CHARLES: And I wish we'd let him change it and have done with it! I wish he'd never lived to see his own family – he wasn't fooled for one moment. He cursed me. Understand? We switched him off and now he's –

MA: We didn't kill him.

CHARLES: No, we did worse. We broke his spirit.

MA: You know I couldn't have harmed a hair of his head... I don't know how you can even... (*Crumples.*)

CHARLES: (*Faltering.*) I know, Ma... I'm sorry. I didn't mean to –

MA: (*Fiercely.*) You want to know how his spirit was broken? I'll tell you what broke his spirit. And who! (*Brandishing the book.*) It's all here!

CHARLES: What?

MA: (*Opens the book.*) Listen... (*Reading.*) "The Fall and Nightmare Death In Life Of Britain's Last Good Man Honest and True... Who covet his Birthright? Who poison the fruit in his orchard? Who make mad the beast in his field? Who lurk in back-rooms in Brussels and Bonn, smelling of leberwurst and cheap cigars, cooking the books, licking the ar..." (*Breaking off.*) I do wish he wouldn't use words like that. See for yourself. (*Thrusts the book at CHARLES, who takes it warily.*)

CHARLES: What's this? Da was keeping some sort of journal?

MA: It's all there. In his own words.

CHARLES: (*Leafing nervously through the pages.*) This is your hand-writing.

MA: (*Snatching the book back from CHARLES.*) This is Book Six.

She rummages in her shopping trolley, pulling out: the wig, which she regards with distaste, dropping it back in the bag; then, more books, which she proudly shows to CHARLES.

He has me up all night.

Repacks the books in the trolley, covering them with the wig.

CHARLES: So... What? He... dictates them to you, or what?

MA: He comes to me. Every night for the last two weeks.

CHARLES: Wait a minute. He "comes to you"?

MA: He won't let me sleep.

CHARLES: Because I thought we'd agreed. Da's dead. Buried in the field behind the old cowshed. I thought we were at least agreed on that.

MA: He's dead, but he's not at peace.

CHARLES: Because any day now they're going to be reading the will, and your Miss Meier must've known there was something a bit fishy, though she can't have known what and – well, not to put too fine a point on it, Ma, if we can't even agree that Da is really dead, your Miss Meier is going to start asking some very awkward and personal questions, which I know you're not going to want to hear one bit.

MA: Don't you worry about me, Charlie. I know how to keep Mum. Don't you worry. (*Tugs on the trolley.*) This is not for the likes of Miss Meier. No, Charlie. We'll bide our time and when the time is right you're going to get us the best lawyers money can buy. We're going to get this business sorted out once and for all. When these books see the light of day, when people in this country see how they've been cheated out of what is rightfully theirs –

CHARLES: Ma. Ma. Ma! What on earth are you talking about?

MA: Restitution, my boy. Setting wrongs to rights. Justice. We'll do whatever it takes, for Da's sake. (*Panics.*) You mustn't tell a soul!

CHARLES: I wouldn't dream of telling anyone. People might get the wrong idea.

MA: Not even Jake! If they knew about the books... They'll stop at nothing.

CHARLES: There is no they, Ma. It's just me and you.

MA: You're just like your brother, never want to think ill of anyone. No, this goes all the way to the top. I know who they are, Charlie. It's all here. (*Tugs on the trolley.*) All the evidence we need. (*Whispers.*) He names names.

CHARLES: (*Uneasy.*) Names?

MA: (*Nods excitedly.*) That night they came with the ambulance.

CHARLES: The doctors?

MA: (*Fiercely.*) They were no doctors! They were from the BBC!

CHARLES: (*Beat.*) Gosh!

MA: They weren't trying to save him. They hooked him up to their "mad meat machine" – he calls it. In White City.

CHARLES: White City... (*Pause.*) Gosh, Ma. And you're getting all this from Da? (*She nods.*) But... I don't understand. Why would the BBC conspire to kill Da?

MA: (*Whispers.*) The Jews...

CHARLES: Oh, Ma!

MA: Oh I know you're not supposed to say things like that. I never learned your London ways.

CHARLES: It's not that, Ma. It's just... bollocks.

MA: Who do you think was behind the beef scare? Where our troubles all began! Who do you think doctored the evidence?

CHARLES: (*Wearily.*) Tell me, Ma.

MA: German Jews... "smelling of leberwurst and cheap cigars".

CHARLES: (*Gently.*) Listen, Ma. These last days have been a terrible strain on you. You've got to allow yourself time to grieve...

MA: There's nothing wrong with me.

CHARLES: I know... In some ways it must be a comfort to know he's still with you. It's only natural. But you can't hold on to him like this. You've got to let him go.

Knocking at the front door, off left. They freeze.

MA: It's them. Quick! The lights.

CHARLES: Ma! Pull yourself together. You're letting your imagination –

Knocking, off.

MA: Oh, you are hopeless sometimes.

MA hurries over to switch off the lights.

Darkness. Knocking, off, louder, longer.

CHARLES: (*Whispers.*) Ma? Ma... Where are you?

A torch-beam flashes on, scanning the room, picking out CHARLES' face. He cries out in alarm.

MA: Shhh! Get over here.

CHARLES follows the beam back to MA. Sound of breaking glass, off.

What did I tell you! I'm ready for them. You stand by the lights and when I give the word...

She switches off her torch. Sound of the window being forced open, an intruder bumping into furniture. Another torch-light appears, scanning the hall, then the kitchen, picking out CHARLES and MA.

Now!

Lights snap up on: MA training a shotgun on JAKE – a charismatic, short-haired man, rakishly dishevelled in his country tweeds – holding his torch and staring at her in amazement.

JAKE: Have I got the wrong house?

MA: Jake!

JAKE: Hello, Ma. (*To CHARLES.*) Hi, Bro. (*CHARLES gapes at him.*)

MA: (*Laughing.*) Oh, Jake, you gave us such a fright.

JAKE: Oh yeah – sorry about the window.

MA: Never mind. Charles'll fix it.

JAKE: Couldn't see any lights on. And you've gone and changed the locks.

CHARLES: You know Ma... Best be on the safe side.

MA: What matters is that you've come home. Oh Jake, it's so good to see you. Come here and let me give you a big hug...

JAKE: Careful with that shotgun, Ma.

MA: Oh! You! (*Laughs.*) Charles!

Peremptorily hands CHARLES the gun. He hangs it back on its peg above the stove.

Oh Jake, Jake... (*Bursts into tears, hugging him.*)

JAKE: Don't cry, Ma.

MA: Where have you been? I've been worried sick. Why didn't you call?

JAKE: Sorry, Ma. I was er... indisposed. Couldn't get to a phone.

MA: Don't give me that. They've got phones everywhere these days.

JAKE: Er... Not where I've been.

MA: (*Dabbing her eyes.*) Never mind. What matters is you're here now.

JAKE looks at CHARLES. They hug.

CHARLES: Good to see you, Little Brother.

JAKE: Good to see you too, Even Littler Than Me Little Brother. How's tricks?

CHARLES: Oh, we have our ups and downs. What happened to your hair?

JAKE: (*Feeling his cropped hair.*) Oh yeah – the dreadlocks. Spot of bother with the old Zippo – torched the lot. (*Takes out his lighter.*) Thought it might be God's way of telling me it's time for a change of image.

CHARLES: It suits you. And the outfit.

MA: Better than those old rags he used to wear. I like your hair, but it does make you look awfully thin. Look at him, Charles, he's all skin and bone. I do hope someone's looking after you. Are you sure you've been eating?

JAKE: Come to think of it, I haven't eaten since... (*Thinks.*)

MA: There's some soup on the hob.

JAKE: Bless you, Ma.

MA: (*Going over to the stove.*) Charles?

CHARLES: Not for me, Ma, I've already... (*Off her reproachful look.*) Well, alright, just a mouthful. (*Off JAKE's amused look.*) Why haven't you been eating? Did you run out of money or did you just forget?

JAKE: Between you and me, Bro, the grub in the Bin leaves something to be desired. They seem to go in for a lot of blue jelly. We reckon they were using food-colour to disguise the medication.

CHARLES glances anxiously at MA, who seems not to hear. She busies herself with the soup.

CHARLES: So... You were er...

JAKE: Unavoidably detained.

CHARLES: Oh, Jake! What was it this time?

JAKE: I'm ashamed to say, I er... kicked a copper up the bum.

His shamefaced expression cracks when he catches CHARLES' eye. They both burst out laughing.

CHARLES: Silly bugger. What you want to go 'n' do a stupid thing like that for?

JAKE: Good question. You get a lot of time, in the Bin, to play back the sequence of events, think through all the bad decisions that got you there in the first place. I kept asking myself – what possessed me? And the more I thought about it the more that's what it seemed to be – a form of possession. I was possessed by something bigger than me, something which, for reasons of its own to which I was not party, obliged me to put the proverbial boot into this particular policeman at that particular moment in space and time...

MA: (*Putting bread and plates on the table.*) You remember the Caravan?

JAKE: Black Rock?

MA: I remember when you two found a snake in the sand-dunes.

JAKE: An adder. We bashed it to death with our cricket bats, then skinned it. Remember, Bro? The meat was all wet and pink. Maybe that's where you got the taste for doctoring.

MA: It wasn't an adder. It was a grass-snake. We only said it was an adder. We wanted you to think you were big and strong. (*Goes back to stirring the soup.*)

JAKE: (*To CHARLES.*) How's the farm? Still torturing the old turkeys?

CHARLES: We all have our crosses to bear. Come Christmas, I might call it a day. (*Off JAKE's grin.*) Seriously. I've been giving it a lot of thought.

JAKE: Well you know me, Bro, never could stomach the smell of ammonia. What does Da have to say about it?

MA: (*Clattering cutlery on the table.*) You remember that time he got a bit merry and locked himself in the lav?

JAKE: Uncle Dick had to break down the door and haul him out.

MA: (*Chuckles.*) They were good times. We were happy then. (*Returns to the stove, preparing to pour the soup into bowls.*)

CHARLES: (*To JAKE.*) And this "particular policeman" was just walking along minding his own business.

JAKE: Oh no! He was man-handling an old lady. It was during an action, land occupation and what not.

CHARLES: Ah, yes! The old actions. Still saving the world, eh?

JAKE: (*Assuming his Humphrey Bogart voice.*) "It's a doighty job but somebody's gotta do it!" It's not as if I had time to weigh up the pros and cons of tangling with the short arse of the law. Wasn't till they got me down the station I twigged I was getting the illuminations. Next thing I know I'm under heavy sedation in the Richard Dadd ward.

CHARLES: Why didn't they call us?

JAKE: The police?

CHARLES: Or the hospital.

JAKE: They didn't know who I was. Wasn't too sure myself at the time.

CHARLES: Oh Jake.

JAKE: And I didn't want to worry Ma. She's got enough on her plate.

CHARLES: You can say that again!

JAKE: How is Da?

CHARLES: Da? Yes... (*Tentatively.*) Jake... Da...

MA bustles over with bowls of soup on a tray.

MA: (*Brightly.*) Here we are!

JAKE and CHARLES make approving noises.

I don't suppose it's very nice. Is that enough for you, Charles?

CHARLES: Ma, I did say... (*Off her look.*) It's fine. Smells delicious.

JAKE: Ah! The pottage. (*Off their looks.*) Genesis twenty five? The pottage of lentils. What Esau sold his birthright for. Lots of farting about with a false hairpiece.

Having explained his Biblical reference to his own satisfaction, JAKE commences eating noisily, with gusto. MA and CHARLES exchange nervous looks.

CHARLES: I'm afraid we're not so well up on our Bible.

JAKE: Number One best-seller – in the Richard Dadd ward. One of the loonies lost an eye in a dispute over a Bible.

MA: I didn't know you'd been in hospital.

JAKE: Oh, you know, Ma, my little problem.

MA: I said you were looking thin. Why didn't you tell me?

JAKE: I didn't want to worry you.

MA: I'm your Mother. I've got a right to worry.

JAKE: Sorry, Ma.

JAKE and CHARLES eat in silence under MA's watchful eye.

MA: I know what you get up to, don't think I don't. Are you taking your tablets?

JAKE: Yes, Ma. I'm right as rain now, honest.

MA: Well... The main thing is, we're all together again.

They eat in gloomy silence.

JAKE: He's dead, isn't he?

MA: Who?

CHARLES: (*Shoots MA a filthy look.*) Yes, Jake. Da died two weeks ago. (*He and MA anxiously await JAKE's reaction.*)

JAKE: I thought so... (*Thoughtfully resumes eating.*)

CHARLES: But... how did you –

JAKE: I had a feeling... (*Eats.*) Well, it was a bit more than a feeling actually. Da came to me. (*Eats. MA shivers involuntarily.*) Ma, this is delicious. (*Stops in mid-mouthful.*) I'm sorry. Is this an inappropriate reaction. I'm never sure how to behave in moments like this. When Magic Ripley fell out of his tree at Newbury I couldn't stop laughing. I wouldn't want you to mistake my outward lack of emotional affect as indicative of a lack of care with regard to Da.

MA: You were always his favourite. (*CHARLES shoots her a pained look.*) Of course we went out of our way to treat you both the same. On your birthday, you had to have exactly the same presents.

CHARLES: (*To JAKE.*) How do you mean – he came to you?

JAKE: In a dream. Well it was a bit more than a dream, really, more like lucid dreaming – all part of the illuminations. He was there in his wheelchair, punching out the old phonemes on that voice-box of his, only no sound came out. It was like he was punching the messages straight into my brain – like all the data in this frolicking gynormous computer being downloaded into my brain – and I knew if I could just make sense of it...

He resumes eating. MA and CHARLES struggle to control their alarm and impatience.

CHARLES: And?

JAKE: And I couldn't. Couldn't process it. He told me everything I need to know, but I didn't know what to do with the information. Bear in mind, at the time in question, I was totally loop-de-loop.

MA: (*Not wishing to know, rising.*) I'll make up your bed. Would you like a bottle? It's turned quite chilly.

JAKE: Bless you, Ma, a bottle would be divine.

MA: (*To CHARLES.*) You just remember what I told you. (*Pointedly fetches her shopping trolley.*) I don't want you to go upsetting Jake.

MA goes off, dragging the trolley behind her. The brothers exchange knowing smiles.

JAKE: What's with the shopping trolley?

CHARLES: Oh, you know... Ever since Da died...
Hence the new locks.

JAKE: (*Glancing at the locked cupboard.*) So what's she got
hidden away in there?

CHARLES: Oh, I dunno... Some of Da's old things.

JAKE: "The family and its tawdry secrets..." (*Off
CHARLES' look, explaining the quote.*) Some 'sixties
shrink. Or anti-shrink. In those days they were
loopier than the patients. And look where it got us.
(*Musing.*) I did use to wonder about Uncle Dick. I
mean, didn't it ever strike you as odd, two men under
one roof?

CHARLES: Nothing odd about that – especially in
those days. They were brothers. Dick helped Da on
the farm.

JAKE: Poor old Ma! She must've been quite cut up
when he died.

CHARLES: Da?

JAKE: Him too... No I was talking about Dick.
Sometimes I think she married the wrong brother.
Don't look so shocked, Charlie! He cared for her
more than Da ever did.

CHARLES: (*Uneasy.*) Jake... Uncle Dick has been dead
for twenty-three years. (*Choosing his words carefully.*)
We were kids. We didn't know what was going on.

JAKE: We had our suspicions. (*An edgy silence.*) But
you're right, I'm sorry. We were talking about Da.

CHARLES: I must say, you do seem to be taking it very
calmly.

JAKE: What can you do? We knew it was only a matter
of time. Suppose I'm too late for the funeral.

CHARLES: Thursday last.

JAKE: Typical. Da used to say I'd be late for my own. Now that does upset me, despite all appearances to the contrary. I'd like to have said goodbye.

CHARLES: Maybe you did, when he came to you...

JAKE: In my dreams! No evading the issue, I screwed up royally. Which is ironic really, because at the time I was labouring under the delusion that I was the Prince of Denmark....

CHARLES: Don't be so hard on yourself, Little Bro. You weren't to know.

JAKE: Oh but I were, Even Littler Than Me Little Bro. I were to know.

CHARLES shifts awkwardly. JAKE becomes sombre.

I let them down, Charlie.

CHARLES: It was easy for me, they let me get on with it. Da pinned all his hopes on you.

JAKE: The firstborn.

CHARLES: By a couple of minutes.

JAKE: Did you come out clinging to my heel?

CHARLES: Not as far as I... How the heck am I supposed to know? (*Pause.*)

JAKE: How's Ma taking it?

CHARLES: You can see for yourself.

JAKE: She's not looking so good.

CHARLES: She still hasn't come to terms with it. Acts as if he's still with us.

JAKE: He is. (*Off his look.*) In a way. They live on in us.

CHARLES: She thinks he's sending her messages. She's got six books full of some sort of automatic writing. Don't tell her I told you. I tell you, Jake, some of that stuff is really loop-de-loop.

JAKE: More messages from Da, eh? I wouldn't say no to a quick scan.

CHARLES: No Jake! Promise me you won't say anything. It could push her over the –

JAKE: Don't look at me like that, Bro. I'm not here to make trouble.

CHARLES: Anyhow, she never lets them out of her sight.

JAKE: Aha! So that's with the shopping trolley!

CHARLES: Jake! Promise you won't even look in the bag. Promise.

JAKE: Relax, Charlie. I told you. Look at me. I'm a reformed character. What's the matter, Bro? You look so stressed out.

CHARLES: You don't have to live with her.

JAKE: (*Nods sympathetically.*) I can take her in small doses.

CHARLES: You got out when the going was good.

JAKE: I was only taking her advice. (*Mimics MA.*) "You boys want to see the world before you settle down."

CHARLES: You've certainly done that. So what are you going to do now?

JAKE: Dunno. Reckon I'm due a spot of R 'n' R. Then there's the book.

CHARLES: You're writing a book?

JAKE: Yes, I'm researching the Michelin guide to Great British Bins. You know those Victorian Gothic follies they used to build, look like they were designed by the inmates – back in the bad old days when they wanted to keep you banged up. Now they can't get rid of you fast enough, it's all throughput and here's a fiver and – "Excuse me, officer, can you tell me the way to the community". They've even closed Friern Barnet. Mind you, I've seen a lot worse than my recent abode. (*Assuming his Old Boy voice.*) "Oh yes, dear boy, compared to a certain Bin in Goa, the Richard Dadd was home from home." (*Impatiently.*) It's a joke, Bro! Richard Dadd. The painter? Eminent Victorian. Killed his own father. (*PC Plod voice.*) "I reckon it was the name what done it, doctor."

CHARLES: (*Laughs.*) I can't keep up with you. I don't know, Jake, sometimes I envy your life...

JAKE: You wouldn't, Bro, believe me – not if you had to live it.

CHARLES: Sometimes I look at my own life and... (*Shrugs helplessly.*) Good old Charles, so... safe and predictable.. There's you bumming round India, losing your mind – what was I doing?

JAKE: Carving cadavers. Doing the doctoring – no, but you did have a life, Bro. And you gave it up without a second thought, sacrificed your own happiness for the good of the family. Let's not belittle what you did there. When I was fried out of my brains in Goa, you were coming home to take care of Da and Ma.

CHARLES: (*Imitating Jake's Bogart voice.*) "It's a doighty job but..." (*They laugh.*)

JAKE: I suppose in a way that's what I'm doing here – trying to – now.

CHARLES: Taking responsibility.

JAKE: (*Nods.*) Coming home. Too late for Da, of course, but there's still a lot to sort out between me and Ma.

CHARLES: Go easy on her, Jake. She's been through a heck of a lot.

JAKE: (*Muses.*) She certainly had to put up with a lot from him.

CHARLES: (*Nods.*) Those last days...

JAKE: When we were kids. She put up with a lot. Turned a blind eye.

CHARLES: She knew what was going on.

JAKE: She could hardly miss it.

CHARLES: He even invited her to the house.

JAKE: Sexy Sadie?

CHARLES: Ma never complained. Not a word.

JAKE: (*Muses.*) Maybe I should broach the subject.

CHARLES: Sexy Sadie?

JAKE: And Uncle Dick. Might help to get it off her chest.

CHARLES: No, Jake!

JAKE: My new therapist's a great believer in the talking cure.

CHARLES: (*Firmly.*) Jake. No.

MA breezes in, dragging her shopping trolley.

MA: I'll do your bottle. How was the soup?

JAKE proudly shows his bowl, wiped clean with bread. At a look from MA, CHARLES dutifully spoons in another mouthful. She fills a hot-water bottle from the kettle on the stove. Silence.

JAKE: It's good to be home.

MA: It's good to have you, dear. The house has been so cold since your poor Da... (*Silence.*) I can't help wishing one of you had given me grandchildren. (*Sighs.*) Never mind. Let's talk about something happier. We're together again. That's all that matters. (*Awkward silence. To CHARLES.*) Did you tell him?

CHARLES: Tell him what?

MA: You know what.

CHARLES: What?

MA: You know.

CHARLES: Not now, Ma. He's only just arrived. Give him a chance to settle in.

MA: Better have it all out in the open.

CHARLES: Everything?

JAKE: If I could just come in here as an impartial observer... (*To CHARLES.*) What exactly is the You Know What what Ma wants you to tell me?

CHARLES: The will.

JAKE: (*Beat.*) Da's will?

MA: Charles gets the farm.

CHARLES: He did provide for you. There'll be a modest trust fund.

JAKE: Modest being the operative word?

CHARLES: Well, he had a few stocks and shares, but most of his savings went on the voice-box, and what with death-duties and solicitors' fees...

A tense pause. They watch him digest the information.

JAKE: (*Shrugs philosophically.*) Pretty much what I expected. Well, it's obvious you get the farm, you're the manager, and manage very well you do too if you don't mind me saying. (*Off their relieved looks.*) So what's with the big build-up? You can't have thought I'd be jealous of you getting the... (*Laughs.*) What would I do with it? I wouldn't know one end of the cow from the udder. (*Off their spooked looks.*) What's the matter? You used to laugh at my jokes.

CHARLES: I'm just relieved that you see it like that, Bro. We weren't sure how you'd take it.

JAKE: Ma's right. Best to have it all out in the open. So that's it? What you had to tell me? (*Laughs.*) Well thank God that's all it is.

CHARLES' laugh is a bit forced. MA doesn't laugh. She clutches the hot-water bottle to her chest, shivering.

Yes 'cause I could sense something you know, the minute I stepped in the house. You could almost smell it.

CHARLES: What?

JAKE: Things hidden. Things unsaid, unspoken, unspeakable... Especially in your own family... It's like you pick up all the coded messages... "Tawdry secrets..."

MA: (*Blurting out.*) Look, can we just talk about something happy!

CHARLES and JAKE spring to her aid.

CHARLES: Ma!

JAKE: What is it, Ma? You're shivering.

MA: I'm alright. I don't know. I hope I'm not catching a chill.

CHARLES: You should go to bed. Come on...

MA: I just want us all to be happy.

CHARLES: We are, Ma. I'm happy. Jake's come home.
We're both happy.

JAKE: Believe me, Ma, I've never been happier.

CHARLES: (*Leading her gently but firmly.*) Ma...

MA: (*Shaking him off, exasperated.*) Alright, Charles! I'm
not an old woman. (*She shuffles towards the hall,
dragging her trolley, stops.*) And don't you boys sit up all
night talking. Jake's tired, aren't you darling.

JAKE: To be honest, Ma, all this excitement... I feel
quite fizzy...

MA: Have you taken your tablet?

JAKE: Not yet, Ma. I take it before I go to bed.

CHARLES: But if you don't go to bed you'll never take it.

JAKE: I said I'll take it later, okay?

MA: Boys! Now don't fight. (*Kissing JAKE.*) Goodnight,
darling. (*Kissing CHARLES.*) Don't you go keeping
him up. (*Glances at his soup bowl.*) Don't you like the
soup?

CHARLES: No – Yes! It's –

JAKE: A triumph, Ma!

MA: (*To CHARLES.*) I hope you're going to finish it.

MA goes off, trundling her trolley.

JAKE: (*In his MA Voice.*) Eat up, Charles! Finish your
mess of pottage.

He laughs. CHARLES pushes away the bowl.

Lights fade.

Scene 3

An hour later. The field behind the old cow-shed. A distant church clock strikes midnight. From inside the cow-shed comes the muffled murmur of sleeping turkeys. A shaft of light from the farmhouse reveals Da's freshly dug grave. Enter JAKE carrying a spade, whistling nonchalantly. He leans on the spade, addressing the grave.

JAKE: Hi, Da. How's tricks? Sorry I didn't make it to the funeral. I got your message but it got through too late. You old bugger, you might have hung on for a couple more weeks. Now we'll never know. No use leaving messages for Ma. She'll just sit on them, drive herself batty. Da... I'm sorry I dropped out of Cambridge. I didn't mean to let you down. I was just trying to find my own way. Traveller's motto, Da – you have to get lost to get found. Especially when you don't know where you're going. And now it's too late. Now I'll never... Never say never, eh Da? That's what you'd say. You're still around here somewhere. I can feel it. Come back to haunt me? Feel free, Da. You're not the first ghost to bugger with my brain. Da? Da!

A powerful torch-beam shines on his face, blinding him.

Enter CHARLES, shining the torch on JAKE.

CHARLES: Jake?

JAKE: Oh... Hiya, Bro.

CHARLES: What's going on here then?

JAKE: Oh... Only me... And Poor Yorick, my man of infinite jest.

CHARLES: Bit late to be paying your last respects.

JAKE: Better late than never.

CHARLES: I didn't mean it like that. I meant... It's after midnight!

JAKE: An unmarked grave in the field behind the cow-shed... It's what he would've wanted.

CHARLES: It was in the will.

JAKE: Laid to rest in the family plot. With old Uncle Dick...

CHARLES: He was quite specific.

JAKE: Good old Da – leave nothing to chance. Did you bury his box?

CHARLES: You mean... *in* a box? A coffin.

JAKE: His voice-box.

CHARLES: Oh that! Er, no... I think it went in the cupboard...

JAKE: Do you mind if I have it? As a memento.

CHARLES: I don't think that's such a good idea.

JAKE: You never know – might be a bit of him left in there.

CHARLES: It'd only upset you.

JAKE: No I mean really – he may have left us some recordings.

CHARLES: Without Da, it's just a heap of old scrap.

JAKE: Some clue... Don't you ever wonder what really happened that night... We do know Da was out late, and Dick went to look for him. Who's to say they didn't meet up? They could have been standing right here, having their man to man, when suddenly, without warning, Da ups and whacks him with his spade –

CHARLES: Jake! Why in God's name would Da want to murder his own brother?

JAKE: Well, that's what we thought at the time.

CHARLES: We were ten years old!

JAKE: We've already got him at the scene of the crime. He had the means. He may well have had the motive...

CHARLES: You must be – (*Checks himself.*)

JAKE: Crazy? I am. I've got a certificate to prove it.

CHARLES: Dick was drunk. He tripped and bashed his head on a rock.

JAKE: (*Adopting a serious tone.*) I've been meaning to ask you, Charles – I mean you're the *doctor* in the house. What do you think? Am I manic depressive or borderline psychotic?

CHARLES: I don't think labels are very helpful here, Jake.

JAKE: Could very helpful to me.

CHARLES: Have you taken your librium?

JAKE: Yes, doctor! (*Sighs.*) I've got it right here. (*Ferreting in his pockets.*) Somewhere... Dr McKee reckons it could be hereditary – a gene for manic depression – in which case I must've got it from Ma.

CHARLES: She is a bit of a mad old bat. And then the whole business with Da...

JAKE: I sometimes think that's why Da loved me most. Because I take after Ma. What do you think?

CHARLES: Not too sure about that, Jake. Must admit I find that idea vaguely...

JAKE: Obscene? Like imagining them having sex?
Well? They must have done it at least once or we
wouldn't be here to wonder at it. Don't you ever
worry about yourself? (*Off his look.*) No, I mean, we're
fifty percent identical, genetically speaking. You
could be carrying my manic gene. What if you have
kids?

CHARLES: I really don't think this is the time or place
for this conversation.

JAKE: Oh, don't misconstrue, Bro. I'd be willing to
wager you got all the common-sense genes. I reckon
I wound up with enough loopy receptors for the both
of us.

CHARLES: So what's with the spade?

JAKE: Anyhow, I can't quite swallow chemicals being
the whole picture. Mrs Khan, she's my new therapist,
she reckons a lot of my problems are rooted in
childhood. Says I should try to sort out my relationships with Ma and Da.

CHARLES: (*Beat.*) What are you doing with that spade?

JAKE: This? A prop, dear boy. A mere prop. (*Leaning on
the spade, as Hamlet.*) "Where be your gibes now? your
gambols? your songs? your flashes of merriment?" (*Off
his look.*) It's all right for you, Bro. At least you had a
chance to say goodbye.

CHARLES: You said goodbye to him. That's what your
dream was all about.

JAKE: Mrs Khan doesn't agree. She says it means
there's still a lot of unresolved issues between me and
Da.

From inside the shed: an eerie rustle of feathers.

CHARLES: Look, if it makes you feel any better, I never had the big heart-to-heart. I don't know if anyone ever does really... I mean, I did try. When it first struck – when you could still take him out and about – I took him to watch Hampshire play. I thought – eight hours without Ma, just me and him – plenty of time to talk through, you know – all the things you want to say. And then, when we were both sitting there... I didn't know where to begin. I mean what do you say? "Look, Da, we both know you're going to die."

JAKE: That's what I'd've said.

CHARLES: Well maybe that's the difference between us. It just seemed selfish, like I was doing it for me, not for him, that he wasn't ready to deal with it, didn't even want to think about it.

JAKE: So what did you do?

CHARLES: Nothing. Just sat and watched the cricket. (*JAKE shakes his head.*) And in the afternoon he fell asleep.

JAKE: Well then, you did, in your own way. You made your peace.

CHARLES: If only you knew! (*Shivers.*) Are you coming in?

JAKE: You go on ahead, Bro. I'll tarry awhile with Yorick here.

CHARLES: Give me the spade, Jake. (*Makes to take the spade.*)

JAKE: (*Resisting.*) Why?

CHARLES: (*Tussling for the spade.*) Just – give me the bloody spade – and – we'll say – no more – about – it!

JAKE: (*Resisting more forcefully.*) For God's sake, Bro! Will you stop fussing over me. You're worse than Ma.

The rustle of feathers builds to the thrum of wings.

CHARLES: You're not digging him up.

JAKE: Who?

CHARLES: Da!

JAKE: Who said anything about digging him up? Can't a feller stroll upon a midnight clear?

Wresting the spade from CHARLES, raising it as if to strike.

Without interfering siblings –

CHARLES: (*Sharply calling him to order.*) Jake! (*Gently.*) We both know what happens when you get over-excited and forget to sleep, don't we? We know how it always ends.

The whirr of beating wings subsides.

JAKE: (*Lowers the spade, relaxing.*) You're right, Bro. Let sleeping turkeys lie. Now where's my librium? (*Pulls out a pill.*) See? Always carry one for emergencies. (*Swallows it.*) Okay, Doc? Come on. It's way past our bed-time. Ma'll be having kittens. (*Walking them off.*) See? You mustn't start jumping to conclusions. I told you. I'm a reformed character.

They go off to the farmhouse. The light is switched off.

Darkness.

An owl hoots.

Scene 4

The farmhouse kitchen. A week later. MA and CHARLES, both wearing formal black, setting the table with bread, cheese and wine.

CHARLES: As far as I can see, he's come home full of good intentions.

MA: The road to Hell is paved –

CHARLES: Oh I know all about that, believe you me! I'm saying, as far as I can make out, he has no hidden agenda. He's taken it all at face value. Obviously he's intuitive enough to sense that something's up – let's face it, Ma, you and I are hardly the most subtle conspirators...

MA: You can always tell when he's up to no good – even when he was a nipper – he gets that butter-wouldn't-melt-in-his-mouth... (*Panics, gripping his arm.*) You didn't tell him about the Books?

CHARLES: 'Course not! Go easy on him, Ma. He's doing his best. He came back to try and patch it up with you.

MA: I never fell out with Jake. I can't help worrying...

CHARLES: (*Calming her.*) I know...

MA: When I think of the nights I've lain awake –

CHARLES: He's doing his best, Ma...

MA: Sometimes I think God must want to punish me.

CHARLES: He's making a real effort. (*MA shakes her head.*) I'm surprised how calmly he seems to be taking it.

MA: The lull before the storm.

CHARLES: Oh, Ma. You're turning into Granny Grimm.

MA: Huh! The day one of you makes me a Granny... Is he taking his tablets?

CHARLES: Yes... Well, as far as I know. I can't stand over him.

MA: You know the signs, as well as I do. All this dressing up like the Lord of the Manor... And have you seen his latest get-up?

CHARLES: No, but... tonight's different. It's only natural he's a bit wired-up. He's got a date.

MA: Huh... Funny time to bring a young lady home to meet the family I must say – and us in mourning. Who is she anyhow? Where's he been hiding her?

CHARLES: He only met her last night.

MA: You don't meet young girls in this neck of the woods.

CHARLES: In the Hart and Trumpet.

MA: Huh! We all know the sort of girl you meet there.

CHARLES: Ma!

MA: What if they're using her to get at him?

CHARLES: Oh, not "Them" again! If I were you, Ma, I'd keep quiet about them. Especially tonight. We don't want our guest to get the wrong idea.

JAKE: (*Off.*) Which idea is that, then?

Enter JAKE, magnificently groomed in evening dress with a slightly oversized dinner-jacket.

CHARLES: Is that Da's old dinner jacket?

JAKE: Hmm... Not a bad fit, eh? If I can't step into the old man's shoes, I might at least try to fill his DJ. Hope you don't mind, Ma?

MA: You look very nice, dear, very dashing.

JAKE: So what's the big idea she mustn't get?

CHARLES: You're certainly going out of your way to impress her.

JAKE: You know these young fillies. Chap's got to make an effort. She's already had my amazing telescopic dong impression.

He performs a mime that would be obscene were it not for the schoolboyish glee with which he does it.

MA: (*Pointedly not seeing him, busying herself with bread and plates.*) Charles was telling me how you met her in the pub...

JAKE: The old Tart and Strumpet. She's not that sort of gal, honest Ma. Good breeding, child-bearing hips – you'll like her, Ma, I promise you. (*Looks nervously at his watch.*) She'll be here any minute. No this is not your common-and-garden Tart-and-Strumpet. This is my betrothed, love of my life, the gal I shall marry, my Bride-To-Be.

Stunned silence. JAKE fits a cigarette into an antique cigarette holder.

CHARLES: Whoa! Whoa, old pal! I think we're putting the cart before the horse here. Girlfriend is one thing, but marriage? You only met her last –

JAKE: I don't mess about, Bro. Straight in there, buy her a drink, pop the question. (*Off their shocked looks, laughing.*) You think I'm winding you up! It's true! I knew, you see – the moment I saw her – I knew.

MA: You don't know the first thing about her.

JAKE: I know I love her, Ma, and she loves me...

MA: Oh, Jake... What are we going to do with you...

JAKE: So. If we could all please at least *try* to behave like a normal family.

CHARLES: Jake, I really think we should discuss this...

JAKE: (*Lights his cigarette, very debonair.*) Frankly, Charles, I don't think there's anything to discuss...

Sound of a car pulling into the yard, off.

That'll be her. You're going to love her, Ma – promise!

He strolls off through the hall. Noises off: JAKE opening the front door, greeting his beloved, canoodling.

MA: (*Whispers.*) What did I tell you?

CHARLES: What can I say, Ma?

MA: A mother knows these things.

JAKE: (*Off.*) Come and meet the folks.

He leads in CLAUDETTE, the dowdy solicitor transformed into a ravishing beauty in a fabulous evening dress.

Ma... Charles... Claudette...

CLAUDETTE smiles sweetly. MA and CHARLES gape at her, dumbstruck. Blackout.

End of Act One

ACT TWO

A minute later. CLAUDETTE sits in the solitary armchair with MA on a chair facing her. JAKE pours wine. CHARLES hovers nervously, trying to avoid eye-contact with CLAUDETTE.

MA: Meier... That's a funny name, dear.

CLAUDETTE smiles quizzically. An embarrassed silence.

JAKE: I suppose it is euphonically intriguing... (*Off their looks.*) The Maya. Astral technicians. Into time travel and what not.

CLAUDETTE: My grandfather was German.

MA: Oh... How interesting. German Jew, was he dear?

CHARLES: Ma!

MA: What's wrong with German Jews? (*To CLAUDETTE.*) My sons are always afraid I'll show them up. Between you and me, Claudette, I think they're secretly ashamed of me.

CLAUDETTE: Surely not?

MA: They're both went to the grammar school – my husband and I went out of our way to give them a good education. I'm just simple farming stock. I never learned to speak properly.

CLAUDETTE: You speak very well.

MA: It's nice of you to say so, dear, even if you don't mean it.

CLAUDETTE: If I didn't mean it, I wouldn't say it –

MA: (*Sighs.*) Anyway, I'm afraid you'll just have to take us as we are.

JAKE: (*Handing out glasses of wine.*) WYSIWIG... (*Off their looks.*) What you see is what you get.

CLAUDETTE: I was sorry to hear about Mr Crow.

MA: It comes to us all, dear. It was a blessing, when it finally came.

CLAUDETTE: I'm sure it was.

MA: Oh Claudette, if you could've seen him!

CLAUDETTE: (*Choosing her words carefully.*) I've heard a lot about him, from Jake.

MA: Jake takes after him. Both headstrong. I'm so glad we've finally got to meet.

CLAUDETTE: Finally? Jake and I only –

MA: That's right, you only met last night. I'm sorry. Getting a bit absent-minded in my old age. Yes he was telling us how you met in the whatyoumacallit –

JAKE: Tart and Strumpet.

MA: Hark at him, Claudette! Cheeky monkey! I do hope you'll take him in hand.

CLAUDETTE: (*Trying not to laugh.*) I'll do my best.

MA: Even I know what it's called. Your local, is it dear?

JAKE: That's the amazing thing! It was her first time.

CLAUDETTE: I don't normally go in for pubs.

JAKE: Fate – or what?

CLAUDETTE: I'd had a particularly heavy day at work.

JAKE: Claudette's a solicitor. Works for old Matheson.

CLAUDETTE: I just wanted to sit down and go through my papers.

JAKE: I'm there in the snug, shooting the breeze with the old timers. Suddenly, out of nowhere, door opens and in wafts this ravishing vision of female pulchritude –

CLAUDETTE: (*Egging him on.*) And what do you do?

JAKE: What any self-respecting red-blooded Englishman would do. I step right up and sweep you off your feet.

CLAUDETTE: He did too. Before I can stop him he's ordering champagne.

JAKE: Only the best for my little Legal Eagle.

CLAUDETTE: Next thing I know he's popping the question. (*To JAKE.*) What was it you said?

JAKE: (*Modestly.*) Oh, something along the lines of: "Madam, your whim is my command. Shall I slay dragons or roger you senseless?"

He's replaying the seduction to CLAUDETTE, who squeals with delight. She seems suddenly animated, uninhibited.

Or words to that effect... (*Resuming the replay.*) "And not to beat about the bush, Madam, with your permission and your father's blessing, I propose to make you my wife."

CLAUDETTE: (*Radiant.*) I'd been waiting all my life for a man to say that to me.

CHARLES: And what did *you* say?

CLAUDETTE: What *could* I say?

CHARLES: Well... You might've said: "I've heard some lines in my time –"

CLAUDETTE: I said I'd think about it.

JAKE: What she really said was: "I'll *drink* about it."

CLAUDETTE: (*Giggles.*) By the third glass I had to admit he'd bowled me over.

JAKE: (*Cheerfully ignoring CHARLES' frantic looks.*) The bubbly... Oh Ma, you'd've been so proud of me. I only wish you and Charles could've been there –

MA: I am proud of you, dear, whatever you do. I'm your mother.

JAKE: (*Reflects.*) Then again, it might've cramped my style. If you had been there, it wouldn't have been real. I'd've been performing in a way – for your benefit.

CHARLES: Isn't that what you're doing here?

JAKE: What – now? (*Considers.*) Well, I suppose in a way – but this is after the event, a reconstruction.

CLAUDETTE: (*To JAKE.*) Like on Crimewatch?

They laugh.

MA: Our Jake could always charm the pants off anyone.

CLAUDETTE: He didn't get that far!

JAKE: Not in the bar!

CLAUDETTE: That was later.

JAKE: In the cornfield.

They both stop, shocked at what they're saying, look at each other, then burst out laughing.

CLAUDETTE: I'm sorry, Mrs Crow.

MA: Call me Ma, dear, everyone else does.

CLAUDETTE: I don't want you to think I make a habit of –

MA: I don't think anything, dear. Call me Ma. You're family now. If Jake had given us some warning, I could've cooked you a nice supper. Would you like some bread and cheese?

JAKE: Or caviar? Bread and caviar.

CHARLES gives him a funny look. MA ignores him.

MA: Did I hear Jake say you worked for Mr Matheson?

CLAUDETTE: Yes. I hear he was a friend of Mr Crow's.

JAKE: Family solicitor.

MA: I'm surprised we haven't met before.

CLAUDETTE: (*Meeting her gaze with a sweet smile.*) So am I.

MA: Jake, why don't you go and show Claudette the garden?

JAKE: (*Baffled.*) It's dark, Ma. There's nothing to see.

MA: (*Chuckles.*) Hark at him! Lazy sausage. (*To JAKE.*) Take a torch. Claudette's dying to see my roses, aren't you dear?

CLAUDETTE: Er... (*Off JAKE's look.*) Perhaps later.

CHARLES: You could always show her your room.

CLAUDETTE: Oh yes! Go on Jake!

JAKE: There's not much to see. It's the guest-room really. I only sleep there when I'm here. Assuming it's semantically viable to be both here and there in the same construction.

CLAUDETTE: (*To CHARLES, gushing.*) He can make words mean whatever he wants them to.

CHARLES: Like Humpty Dumpty.

JAKE: "The question is – who is to be master."

CLAUDETTE looks from one to the other, not getting the 'Alice' reference, momentarily out of her depth.

CHARLES: (*Beat.*) Alright then. You be It. Give her the Grand Tour.

JAKE: (*To CLAUDETTE.*) You want to see the ancestral pile?

CLAUDETTE: Oh yes! I'd love to have a little look round. How old is the farmhouse?

CHARLES: Close on three hundred years.

MA: You can't go in the attic. It's locked.

CHARLES: The roof's leaking.

JAKE: How does locking the door help with a leaky roof?

CHARLES: The floor-boards are rotten. It's not safe. It's been that way for months. We can't afford to fix it.

JAKE: Is the cupboard leaking? (*Rattles the padlocked door to the cupboard.*)

MA: (*Sharply.*) You stay away from there!

JAKE: So why the lock?

MA: It's none of your business!

CHARLES: Jake! Back-off, okay.

JAKE: Only I wouldn't want Claudette to think there were any skeletons in our cupboards.

MA: She doesn't think anything of the kind. Do you, dear?

CLAUDETTE: Why should I?

JAKE: So I'd be quite wrong to infer any correlation between locks and leaks?

CHARLES: (*Firmly.*) Don't even think about it.

JAKE: Is it something to do with this wrong idea she mustn't get?

CHARLES: It's nothing to do with anything! Look don't just stand there asking stupid questions. There are plenty of other rooms to show her.

MA: I'd prefer it if you didn't go in my room. (*To JAKE.*) I don't want Claudette seeing all my dirty vests. (*To CLAUDETTE.*) I'm afraid you'll have to excuse the mess. Jake gave us no warning.

CHARLES: Ma! Let them go.

JAKE: Madam... (*Escorts CLAUDETTE out to the hall, every inch the gallant.*) The hallway...

They disappear from view. MA and CHARLES are left listening to them making merry in the hall.

This here's the Crow rutting stone.

CLAUDETTE: (*Laughing, off.*) Oh, Jake! You're incorrigible!

JAKE: Ancient family tradition. At puberty, the male Crows are obliged to roger seven local virgins.

CLAUDETTE: (*Laughs.*) Did *you* have to do it?

JAKE: The dastardly deed? Oh, yes. Charles and I had to take turns. (*She laughs.*) These days the ritual has fallen sadly into disuse. Can't seem to find the virgins.

Their ribald laughter fades as they move off through the house. MA immediately occupies the empty armchair.

MA: (*Calling softly.*) Claudette? (*Listens.*) Little slut! What do we do now?

CHARLES: Whatever we do we mustn't start jumping to conclusions.

MA: Well I'd've thought it was obvious, even to you!

CHARLES: Do you think she recognised me? Without my wig. (*Off MA's look.*) Well alright, of course she's on to us – although you and I know she doesn't know the half of it.

MA: What are you wittering on about? She knows enough doesn't she? How much more does she have to know?

CHARLES: Alright, let's assume she knows there was some skull-duggery, some cack-handed attempt to stop him changing his will. What's she going to do? I mean it's not as if we forged it.

MA: She can have it declared null and void.

CHARLES: She could try. But she wouldn't exactly come out smelling of roses. Da wanted it done there and then – he couldn't have been more explicit. And she chose to ignore her client's instructions. We could even sue her for negligence.

MA: That's a point!

CHARLES: The fact is, we don't know *what* she's up to. If she'd wanted to she could've come right out with it, the minute she clapped eyes on us. She didn't say anything.

MA: Why should she? She knows she's got us where she wants us.

CHARLES: Yes, but I get the distinct impression she hasn't said anything to Jake –

MA: Huh! She's got him wrapped round her little finger –

CHARLES: You can see he has no idea what's going on. He seems more concerned about your flipping cupboard.

MA: I expect she's telling him right this minute. That's why she was so keen to let him show her around – "I'd love to take a little look round" – I bet she would, the crafty cow!

CHARLES: You were the one desperately trying to get rid of them. The garden!

MA: And did you see the way she jumped at it?

CHARLES: Well whatever *she's* up to, I swear Jake's completely innocent. He's chasing a dream –

MA: Like a lamb to the slaughter.

CHARLES: I'm saying we should at least consider the possibility that this is precisely what it seems – two young people in love... (*Off her look.*) Well look at them, Ma – so happy, so alive.

MA: If you can't see the signs.

CHARLES: Oh I know, his manic phase. Even so, we don't want to rain on his parade. I can't help feeling he's in touch with something real.

MA: Dirty little bitch. Can't wait to get her hands on his money.

CHARLES: What money?

MA: Your money! Wake up, boy! You really believe it just so happened, after a hard days work, she just happens to "waft" into the Hart and Trumpet? She followed him in! They've been planning this for weeks. They were following him.

CHARLES: (*Patiently.*) Ma. We've got to try to keep this in perspective. We haven't broken any laws. (*Reflects.*) Well, not as far as I –

MA: You're going to have to negotiate.

CHARLES: Negotiate? With Clau –

MA: Get her alone, talk to her, find out what she wants.

CHARLES: And then?

MA: Take care of it. Buy her off, seduce her, whatever it takes.

Sounds of JAKE and CLAUDETTE coming downstairs, laughing in the hall.

CHARLES: Ma! We're talking about Jake's fiance. Anyhow, I can't seduce to order.

MA: Oh you're hopeless. If only your Da were here. I'll talk to her. You get rid of Jake.

CHARLES: How am I going to –

MA: Use your imagination.

Enter JAKE and CLAUDETTE, somewhat dishevelled but glowing, behaving like naughty children. MA turns on her sweetest smile.

Claudette.

CLAUDETTE: I had no idea it was so big... (*Suppresses a giggle.*) And rambling...

JAKE: I told you, it's huge.

CLAUDETTE: (*The giggle erupts.*) Sorry.

JAKE: I've just initiated her into the mysteries of the Crows.

MA: Would you like some bread and cheese? I'm sorry there's nothing better to offer...

JAKE: There's the caviar.

MA: (*Ignores him.*) But, as you can see, we are in mourning.

Her remark shames JAKE and CLAUDETTE into silence. A long awkward silence.

JAKE: There really is caviar. In the scullery. And –
(*Laughs.*) What am I thinking? The bubbly!

CHARLES: (*Frowns.*) Champagne?

CLAUDETTE: Oh I don't know. That wine really went
to my head.

CHARLES: Champagne, Jake?

JAKE: Do us a favour, Bro, it's in the scullery with the
Ruski fish-eggs.

CHARLES: So why don't you get it?

JAKE: Don't be like that, Bro. As a matter of fact, I was
hoping you'd agree to be my best man.

CHARLES: Tell you what, Jake. Why don't we discuss it
in the scullery?

JAKE: You want we both go?

CHARLES: You can show me what you've got.

JAKE: In the scullery?

CHARLES: And explain how you got it.

JAKE: Man to man?

CHARLES: And where we go from here.

JAKE: Leave the ladies to their own devices.

CHARLES: That's the general idea.

JAKE: Right ho! I expect you girls could do with a nice
cosy little chat, what? (*To CLAUDETTE.*) Excuse me,
dearest. Duty calls. My best man, to be precise.
Think he wants to tell me the facts of life.

CHARLES hustles JAKE off to the scullery.
CLAUDETTE drops her excitable schoolgirl act. She sits
in a chair facing MA, steadily holding her gaze, smiling.

MA: So... Claudette...

CLAUDETTE: Ma...

MA: Don't you Ma me! (*Catching herself, smiles.*) Yes. Why not? Family... Assuming you two are serious about getting married? Only I wouldn't want to think you were stringing him along. Jake's a very sensitive boy, and so trusting – it would never occur to him that some people might have interior motives, that they might be looking to take advantage.

CLAUDETTE: Look, I only met him last night – (*Silenced by MA's derisive laugh.*)

MA: Look, dear, we both know what all this is about. So why don't we stop all this fiddle-dee-dee...

CLAUDETTE: What is this all about? Tell me, Ma.

MA: It's not what you think.

CLAUDETTE: To be perfectly honest, Ma, I don't know what to think.

MA: Of course not. How could you?

CLAUDETTE: I only know what I saw.

MA: You don't. You might think you do, but you couldn't have known what you were seeing.

CLAUDETTE: I do know there's something not quite right here.

MA: You don't know the history.

CLAUDETTE: In fact, I'd go so far as to say – something very wrong.

MA: If you only knew.

CLAUDETTE: (*Shrugs.*) Tell me.

MA: Whatever we did, believe me Claudette, it was for his own good.

CLAUDETTE: I see.

MA: You don't. You don't see. How could you?

CLAUDETTE: (*Sighs.*) Once again, you put me in a very delicate position. On the one hand, there are questions of professional confidentiality –

MA: There's that too!

CLAUDETTE: On the other, there's Jake.

MA: You think if you marry Jake you'll get the farm!

CLAUDETTE: (*Laughs.*) So that's what you think! (*Considers.*) Well, yes, as things stand, there certainly are grounds for Jake to contest the will.

MA: You just try! You'll be sorry, my girl!

CLAUDETTE: Then again, as Jake's prospective spouse and beneficiary, my own position is, shall we say, severely compromised.

MA: Ha ha! Yes! You didn't think of that.

CLAUDETTE: But I did. (*Laughs.*) And you're way ahead of me. The thought of contesting the will hadn't even crossed my mind. No, my principal concern is my professional responsibilities. As your solicitor I would advise you that the will may turn out to be the least of your worries.

MA: What are you driving at?

CLAUDETTE: It may even be a police matter.

MA: So that's your little game! You picked the wrong woman to blackmail, my dear! I'll fight you all the way, I'll – I'll sue you for negligence! Ha ha! Yes! You mark my words, things'll come up in court... (*Checks herself.*) You can't even imagine. (*Pause.*) You want money? Talk to Charles.

CLAUDETTE: (*Laughs.*) You'd make a lousy poker player.

MA: I'm sure you two can come to some arrangement.

CLAUDETTE: Arrangement! Ma, what do you take me for – some little gold-digger from the Big City? You got me all wrong, Ma.

MA: (*Shouting.*) What do you want?

CLAUDETTE: Right now I want Jake.

MA: He doesn't want you.

CLAUDETTE: How would you know?

MA: I'm his mother.

Enter CHARLES bearing a plate of heaped black caviar.

CHARLES: (*Showing it to CLAUDETTE as if nothing's happened.*) Have to excuse the presentation. So... What's the verdict?

CLAUDETTE: (*Smiles.*) The jury's still out.

MA: Claudette plays poker, don't we dear?

CLAUDETTE: Your mother has some very odd ideas about me.

MA: (*To CHARLES.*) Where is he?

CHARLES: In the scullery. I got him to put the champagne in an ice bucket. He won't tell me where he found the money to –

MA: I hope to God he didn't steal it.

CHARLES: We've got about two minutes.

MA: Tell her.

CHARLES: Tell her what?

MA: You know what. (*Impatiently.*) About Jake! Just tell her the truth.

CHARLES: The whole truth?

CLAUDETTE: So you're in on it too, Charles. Or is it Jake? (*Scrutinizes him.*) No. Not my Jake. I have to say, Charles, you do a pretty poor impersonation. As for that ridiculous wig!

CHARLES: Take it from me, Claudette – you have no idea what's going on here.

CLAUDETTE: Not yet. But I do intend to –

CHARLES: No! You don't! You don't know what you're getting into. Believe me, I know my brother. I've seen him like this before –

CLAUDETTE: I've known him less than twenty-four hours and already he's changed my life. I've never had so much fun. He really knows how to make things happen!

CHARLES: Don't get me wrong, Claudette, I know exactly what you mean. When he gets in his states – illuminations he calls 'em – it's like the whole world is alive with meaning and significance. He'll pick up on a stray word and take it apart – dictionary definitions metaphysical meanings use it as a launch-pad for dazzling verbal pyrotechnics –

CLAUDETTE: He's a poet, a mad poet –

CHARLES: Exactly – but! Even as I envy him, I know, it's a curse – believe me, Claudette. I know. I know what happens when he gets over-excited. I know that for every high there's a great big messy crash to pay and you don't want to see that, you mark my words, for his sake...

CLAUDETTE: Charles... I'm not stupid. I didn't fall for this – Randy Squire routine. I know it's only an act. If it was for real, I couldn't take him seriously. It's all an act, a joke, a mask – don't you see – there's someone inside there – trying to get out.

MA: As if she cared!

CLAUDETTE: (*Defiantly.*) The night he took me in the cornfield – it really was like it's supposed to happen in fairy-tales or in the movies. He made it happen! The moon was full and afterwards he sang to me –

CHARLES: Claudette. There isn't time for all this. If it's about money – well you've seen from the will, it doesn't amount to much... As for the – I mean what use is a farm if there's no-one to farm it? If you care about Jake, take my advice, stay away.

CLAUDETTE: Oh yes, I forgot. It's for his own good.

MA: You're wasting your breath. She doesn't care about Jake. (*To CLAUDETTE.*) If you're not after our money, why are you here?

JAKE: (*Off.*) I invited her, Ma. (*Comes in with a magnum of champagne in an ice-bucket.*) I did tell you. (*To CLAUDETTE.*) She's a bit absent-minded.

MA: Claudette and I were just getting to know one another, weren't we, dear. (*Chuckles.*) Eh, Jake love, I reckon Claudette's not so sure she wants to marry you. Claudette thinks you're a bit of devil.

CLAUDETTE: No, Ma. I think my own thoughts. (*MA scowls.*) Right now, for instance, I'm thinking –

JAKE: Out loud. You're thinking out loud.

CLAUDETTE: So I am! You see, Ma, your son is very perceptive. He's also intelligent, sexy, witty –

JAKE: Am I blushing? See, Ma. She'll make an honest woman of me yet.

CLAUDETTE: So I can't help wondering, Ma, if you don't mind me asking – what exactly is the problem with Jake?

Stunned silence.

JAKE: Is there a problem with me? Because if there is, rest assured dearest, I shall not cease from mental strife –

CLAUDETTE: You're fine, love, just the way you are.

JAKE: Till we have built Jerusalem.

CLAUDETTE: I don't see a problem. Do you, Ma? (*To JAKE.*) It was only that – well, Charles and your Ma here keep alluding to something they apparently envy you for – but it's also a curse? And how I mustn't get you too excited.

JAKE: Oh that? Thought I told you. Yes. Well, I am a bit bonkers.

CLAUDETTE: Oh that! (*To MA and CHARLES, laughing.*) Well I knew that last night, in the cornfield.

CHARLES: He doesn't just mean a bit wild and impulsive.

JAKE: Lucky I told you –

CHARLES: He's has a clinical condition.

JAKE: As it turns out.

CHARLES: He's a manic depressive!

JAKE: Steady on, Bro. (*To CLAUDETTE.*) Didn't expect them to start dragging out the old psychiatric records. Still, makes a change from the photo-album, eh? Expect they think they're doing it for my own good.

CLAUDETTE: Oh they do. You wouldn't believe the things they do for you.

JAKE: (*To MA and CHARLES.*) Well you can both stop worrying about me. I'm pleased to announce that as of last night I can honesty say I am fully and comprehensively cured.

CHARLES: (*Alarmed.*) Cured?

JAKE: Healed. As of last night in the cornfield. Oh, don't get me wrong, Bro, we're not talking about a quick roger in the rye. This is love. The real thing. Her love has healed me.

CHARLES: You mean you've stopped taking your –

JAKE: That's what I'm saying. Who needs 'em?

CHARLES: (*To CLAUDETTE.*) If you have any hand in this –

CLAUDETTE: I think Jake's big enough to make his own decisions.

CHARLES: It's a chemical disorder. He's fine as long as he keeps taking his librium.

JAKE: Librium makes you sick and woozy. I don't want to end up pop-eyed like some of my loony chums.

CHARLES: Jake. You have to –

JAKE: Take responsibility for my own life. Yes! Claudette agrees.

CHARLES: Claudette, if you don't tell him to take his tablet right now, you are going to see something you will very much regret – I promise you! He's already high as a kite. Ma and I can see the signs.

CLAUDETTE: If you're asking me, you and your Ma see what you want to see.

CHARLES: We've seen it all before.

CLAUDETTE: If you really want my opinion, there's nothing wrong with Jake.

JAKE: Nothing the love of a good woman can't fix.

CLAUDETTE: (*Caresses Jake.*) And you have agreed to keep seeing your therapist, haven't you, poppet?

JAKE: Anything you say, my little Legal Eye.

CHARLES: You're playing with fire –

CLAUDETTE: (*Wheeling to face him, sharply.*) No if you want my opinion, it's this family fucked him up.

Shocked silence.

CHARLES: We don't use language like that in this house, Claudette.

JAKE: Er, yes... Easy on the F-word, old girl. Ma doesn't like it.

CLAUDETTE: Oh, yes, sorry, I forgot, mustn't upset Ma, whatever we do.

JAKE: She can be a bit possessive. My therapist says it's perfectly natural with mothers and sons. Well, within reason... Chin up, old girl. You're not the first prospective Bride-to-Be to have a little set-to with the in-laws... (*Cheerfully addressing them all.*) Now come on – as Ma would say – let's all make a big effort to be nice. Chin up, Mum! Why so glum? You're not losing a son... You're gaining a solicitor! (*CLAUDETTE laughs, relaxing.*) Now! Who's for bubbly?

CHARLES: I've still got some wine.

JAKE: (*Cod German voice.*) Wein? Schwein!

Takes his glass, dramatically tossing wine over his shoulder.

For good luck. Come on, this is supposed to be a celebration!

CLAUDETTE is somewhat taken aback by JAKE's eccentric behaviour, but loyally follows suit. CHARLES does the same, without enthusiasm. MA defiantly clutches her glass.

Come on, Ma. For me.

MA peremptorily throws her wine over her shoulder.

That's better.

Removes the champagne bottle from the ice-bucket.

After all, Ma, I'm doing it partly for you. (*MA groans.*) Oh I can see how it might seem a bit much – the old funeral bak'd meats etcetera. (*Fiddles with the cork.*) But that's the whole point. Charles knows how bad I felt about missing Da's funeral. Ever since I got back I've been looking for a way to make amends. Last night, in the cornfield, it all became clear. I didn't plan it. It just happened.

CHARLES: Seems a heck of a lot happened in that cornfield.

His remark seems not to have the desired effect. JAKE and CLAUDETTE cuddle, simpering.

JAKE: When faint heart won fair lady, it had no hidden agenda. Or any agenda come to that! I'd already asked her to marry me, you see, in the bar. It was only later...

CLAUDETTE: In the cornfield...

JAKE: Suddenly it all seemed to fall into place.

CHARLES: Marriage?

JAKE: You know what they say about weddings and funerals.

CHARLES: What do they say, Jake?

JAKE: Bring the family together. Everybody ready? Here we go... (*Pops the cork. Champagne foams. CLAUDETTE cheers. CHARLES joins in, belatedly, half-heartedly.*) This'll soon break the ice. Ma? (*MA proffers her glass mechanically. JAKE pours champagne for all. He taps on his glass, calling for silence.*) Ladies and gentlemen, with your permission I would like to propose a toast. (*Raises his glass.*) The family.

CLAUDETTE: The family. (*Chinks glasses with JAKE.*)

CHARLES: (*Laughs.*) Oh what the hell! The family.
(*Chinking glasses.*) And the best of British luck to you
both.

JAKE: Ma? (*Chinks his glass on hers.*)

MA: (*Muttering.*) Family...

JAKE: Not forgetting absent Elders. (*Toasting.*) The Dick
and the Da.

*MA looks as if she's seen a ghost. JAKE chinks glasses with
CHARLES and CLAUDETTE. They sip champagne.*

CLAUDETTE: Mmm... It's good.

JAKE: The best.

CHARLES: Must've set you back a bit more than
twenty quid.

JAKE: Chill out, Bro! (*Produces a cigar.*) Have a cigar.

MA: Charles doesn't –

CHARLES: (*Taking the cigar.*) Come on, Ma. It's not
every night my brother gets engaged. (*Accepts a light
from Jake.*)

JAKE: Now I'd like to call upon the Best Man to propose
a toast to the Young and Blooming Bride-To-Be.

CLAUDETTE: Oh Jake!

CHARLES: Well, Hell, why not. (*Raises his glass.*)
Claudette. (*They chink glasses.*)

JAKE: Go on, Ma, show there's no hard feelings.

MA: (*Starts.*) Uh...

JAKE: (*Raising his glass to CLAUDETTE.*) My Portia...
(*Aside to CHARLES.*) The lawyer not the car.

CLAUDETTE laughs.

CHARLES: So... Any plans for the honeymoon?

JAKE: (*To CLAUDETTE.*) I was thinking Thailand. There's this place on Ko Pan Gang, Bottle Beach, you can only get there by boat –

CLAUDETTE: Whatever you say, darling. You're the traveller.

JAKE: Not many creature comforts. Hut on stilts, sort of thing.

CLAUDETTE: Sounds heavenly. Get up with the sun...

JAKE: And get down to the serious business of starting a family.

CLAUDETTE: I'm sure we'll find plenty of time for that.

JAKE: Two girls and a boy, Ma.

CLAUDETTE: Oh! I thought it was two boys and a girl.

JAKE: Whatever you say, dearest. You're in charge of that department. What shall we call them?

CLAUDETTE: Why not Jake and Charles.

JAKE: You hear that "Uncle Charles"? What would you say to a little namesake. And Jake junior. And Becky for the girl. That was Ma's name before she became Ma. Oh – unless of course you want a little Claudette?

CLAUDETTE: Becky's a lovely name for a girl.

JAKE: That's settled then. It's funny, Ma, there's you only the other day complaining about not having grandchildren. And here we are already on the job.

MA: (*To CHARLES.*) Ask him where he got the money.

CHARLES: For what? (*Off her pained look.*) I did. He won't tell me.

JAKE: What? Oh, the bubbly. As far as I'm aware, Bro, the bubbly is on the Best Man.

CHARLES: What's that supposed to mean?

JAKE: I mean traditionally. According to the time-honoured laws of matrimonial etiquette.

CHARLES: Jake... I gave you twenty quid to go into the village.

MA: (*To CHARLES.*) You never told me that!

CHARLES: For Heaven's sake, Ma. I couldn't send him off without something in his pocket. (*To JAKE.*) Champagne, caviar, cigars – where d'you get them?

JAKE: France, Russia, Havana –

CHARLES: Jake. I'm serious. (*JAKE grins sheepishly.*) Where did you –

JAKE: Basingstoke.

CHARLES: Jake. I won't ask you again –

JAKE: I got them on credit.

CHARLES: What credit? You haven't got – (*It hits him.*) You took my credit card!

JAKE: Borrowed it. (*CHARLES gapes.*) You've every right to be angry, Charles. To tell the truth, I wish you would. All this holding it in, bottling it up – it's not healthy. Go on, Charlie! Express yourself. Throw a wobbly! Howl! Rage! Hit me if you want to – hit me! But for God's sake, do something!

CHARLES: (*Showing exemplary self-control.*) Is this what you call taking responsibility?

JAKE: (*Conciliatory.*) I was going to tell you, Bro. I knew you wouldn't want to skimp on your duties as Best Man, but you were a bit slow off the mark, so I took the liberty of –

CHARLES: You forged my signature!

JAKE: Pretending to be you.

CLAUDETTE: (*Laughs.*) There's justice! What's the problem, Charles, he's only spending what's rightfully his.

JAKE: Rightful heir to the Crow throne, eh? Well, I suppose according to the rules of primogeniture, I am strictly speaking the firstborn.

CLAUDETTE: (*To CHARLES.*) I'm surprised you didn't tell him yourself, since you only did it all for his own good. (*Beat.*)

JAKE: Did what? (*Looks from one to the other.*) Am I missing something?

CLAUDETTE: You see, Jake, your brother forged more than just your signature.

JAKE: Did he now? Ho ho! (*Looks blank.*) How do you mean?

CLAUDETTE: I've been here before.

JAKE: We all have, if our Hindu friends are to be –

CLAUDETTE: As a solicitor.

JAKE: Believed. (*Puzzled.*) To write the will?

CLAUDETTE: Revise it.

MA: For the umpteenth time! He was obsessed with that blinking will. He didn't know if he was coming or going –

CLAUDETTE: There he is, in his wheelchair, can't even speak for himself without your Ma butting in. All he can do is call for Jake.

JAKE: (*Touched.*) Da asked for me?

CLAUDETTE: He wanted you to have the farm. (*JAKE seems unable to process the information.*) And sure enough, Jake appears, in his rags and dreadlocks, and duly proceeds to renounce his inheritance: "Not me, Da, I'm the black sheep, don't know one end of the cow from the udder."

JAKE: (*Stunned.*) You're saying you saw another Jake.

CLAUDETTE: Precisely.

JAKE: Spooky! Long hair? (*She nods.*) Crusty old rags? (*She nods.*) Another Jake... (*Ponders.*) All I can suggest, m'lady, is that you somehow caught a glimpse of me, as I then was, before I torched my dreadlocks, the premonition of me stumbling blindly towards you through space and time –

CLAUDETTE: (*Laughs, exasperated.*) Jake!

JAKE: You may laugh but... More things in Heaven and Earth, Horatia –

CLAUDETTE: It wasn't you.

JAKE: Not as I am, but as I was.

CLAUDETTE: It was Charles!

JAKE: (*Thoroughly confused, or perhaps not wanting to understand.*) Charles? Er, no... (*Chuckles, aside to CHARLES.*) M'learned friend appears to be labouring under the delusion –

CLAUDETTE: I don't think so.

JAKE: Charles is my brother. We're twins. But not identical.

CLAUDETTE: Jake! You're being perverse. You don't want to –

JAKE: Two Jakes? Wasn't that a remake of Chinatown? The sequel! Which come to think of it Chinatown was all about incestuous goings-on, dirty old men diddling their daughters. Nothing like that in this family, Claudette, I do assure you!

CLAUDETTE: Charles dressed up as you and –

JAKE: Silence, Madam, or I shall be obliged to exercise my male prerogative! Charles? I'm sure there's a perfectly reasonable explanation...

MA: Of course there is.

JAKE: (*Helplessly looking to CHARLES for guidance.*) Bro?

MA: She dreamed up this whole –

CHARLES: No, no. No! That's enough, Ma! I've had enough, do you hear?

Grabs MA's shopping trolley, tussling with her.

MA: (*Resisting.*) Charles! Stop it! What are you –

CHARLES: I think it's – high time – we all – faced up – to a few – home truths!

He snatches the trolley from her, dragging it across the room to unzip it. MA stares in shock as he brandishes the wig.

It's true, Bro.

JAKE: (*Laughing.*) What's this?

CHARLES: What does it look like?

JAKE: False Hairpiece?

CHARLES: It's all true.

JAKE: Jacob and Esau! And boy was E. sore! E. is an
    eyesore... I saw Esau sitting on the see-saw. I saw
    Esau, Esau me! Esau the hairy man, Shaman of the
    open spaces... Then Jacob the tent-dweller fakes call
    of the wild to extract blessing from old blind tribal
    chief... Two nations in thy womb, Ma! Nomads v.
    Settlers. Most basic conflict known to man. (*Sports
    Commentator voice.*) "Into Extra Time, Des, the
    Kikuyu've bought-up all the land but the Masai've
    made off with the cattle. It's War, Des, but not as we
    know it. Now it's Shaman! Shaman neatly nutmegs the
    defender. My word! Still Shaman – penetrating to the
    very heart of the Dominator Culture. Jacob off his
    goal-line, Esau lobs him – GOAL!"

*They all stare at JAKE's manic performance, transfixed.
He appears to relax, draining his glass.*

Well thank God that's sorted. Champagne anyone?
(*Offers CLAUDETTE a refill.*)

CLAUDETTE: When are you going to face facts. Your
    Ma and Charles conspired to steal what is rightfully –

Unseen, MA creeps over to take the shotgun from its peg.

JAKE: Hang on, old thing. They didn't steal it. I sold my
    birthright.

CLAUDETTE: You weren't even here.

JAKE: For a mess of pottage.

CLAUDETTE: They lied to you Jake! Your own family!

JAKE: Just because you've got hairy lips, there's no
    need to talk like a c –

CHARLES: (*Sharply.*) Jake!

JAKE: Ooops! (*Covers his mouth.*) Sorry, Ma.

CLAUDETTE: (*Abruptly.*) I'm going!

MA: You're not going anywhere, my girl!

They all look up to see MA training the gun on CLAUDETTE.

CHARLES: (*Despairing.*) Oh, Ma...

MA: I know who sent you, don't think I don't. Thought they'd use you to get at my Jake. Like they got at him in their hospitals, poisoned his mind with their sex-filth and drugs. (*Off her bewildered look.*) Oh yes, I know who they are. I can name names.

CHARLES: No, Ma... Not that again –

MA: I've been watching you, "Miss Meier", watching your every move. Police matter? I'll see you in court, Miss Meier, in *my* time. Then I'll produce *my* evidence, call *my* witness.

JAKE: Hang about, Ma. You're saying... I was got at?

MA: (*Shaking her head.*) Oh, Jake... Jake...

JAKE: Programmed to destroy my own family? That's awful, Ma.

MA: It's all right, Jake. I won't let them hurt you.

JAKE: (*Hillbilly Voice.*) Looks like we're in this together – huh Ma? So what do we do, Ma, yous and mes, just like hole up in here 'n' all.

MA: That's right, Jake. Nobody goes anywhere until I say so.

JAKE: You want I should barricade the door – huh Ma?

CHARLES: Stop it! Both of you.

JAKE: No – but I am intrigued by this notion that I was somehow got at. I remember when Da came to me in the hospital and was sending me all these messages, it was like someone or something was jamming the transmission. You see? Interference.

CHARLES: Cut it out, Jake! (*Advancing on MA.*) Ma...
Give me the gun, Ma.

MA: (*Aiming at CHARLES.*) Don't make me, Charlie.

CHARLES: It's not loaded. (*Snatches the gun, hangs it back on the peg.*) I took the precaution of removing the shells.

JAKE: Had us worried for a moment there Ma. Now...
What was it? (*Racking his brains.*) The fall – and nightmare... Nightmare Death! Death In Life! Yes... The Books! Yes – he said he would repeat the message, commit it to writing.

MA: (*To CHARLES.*) You told him!

JAKE: It wasn't Charles, Ma. It was Da. He said he'd send them to you for safe keeping – yes and that you were to pass them on to me –

JAKE makes a dash for the shopping trolley. MA runs to intercept him. For an old woman she is remarkably agile and strong. They grapple for the Books. JAKE snatches one, scurrying to the other side of the room. MA crouches, guarding the remaining books. CHARLES and CLAUDETTE watch helplessly, transfixed.

JAKE: (*With the book, reading the title page.*) "Book Seven." (*Looks up, spooked, quoting from the Bible.*)

Revelation, five, two:

"And I saw a strong angel proclaiming with a loud voice: Who is worthy to open the book, and to loose the seals thereof?"

JAKE opens the book.

What have we here? (*Reads.*) "Heal the rift, Jake."
See? Addressed to me in person – look Claudette, my name – right there. (*Shows her. She nods warily. He reads on.*) "Endgame 2000 Big Players in toxic leberwurst and cheap cigars to rig the rip twixt Man

and beast." (*Looks up, puzzled.*) Rig the rip? Or should that be RIP? (*Reads.*) "End war twixt flesh and spirit." (*Scans the page.*) "Flesh and blood." "Kith and kindred...." Old Bugger does tend to repeat himself... (*Selects a new page at random, staring at it, bemused.*) Hey, Bro. Get a load of this. (*Showing CHARLES the book.*) "He has a brother... He has a brother..." Over and over... (*Shivers, laughing.*) Like in The Shining. What do you make of it?

CHARLES: It's her guilt talking. "He has a brother" – the brother she dressed me up in that infernal wig to disinherit – am I right, Claudette?

CLAUDETTE: (*Completely out of her depth.*) Er... That's about the gist of it.

CHARLES: Automatic writing for Christ's sake! – all mixed up with paranoid ravings about a Zionist Conspiracy!

JAKE: (*Musing.*) "He has a brother... He has a brother... He has a..."

MA: (*Blurting out.*) Dick!

JAKE kneels beside her, a child consoling his distraught mother. The others look on in bemused silence.

He was the only one had any time for me. Not that your Da ever took much notice! Too busy with that fancy barmaid of his.

JAKE: (*To CHARLES.*) Sexy Sadie!

MA: (*Lost in her own world.*) But he knew... Right from the word go...

JAKE: (*To MA.*) That's what we used to call her, Sexy –

MA: I'd just given birth... That's when he told me... That's all he said... "I has a brother." Never mentioned it again, but he knew... And he knew I knew he knew...

JAKE: We all knew, Ma! We all did, deep down.

MA: It was Dick!

JAKE: I know. Uncle Dick. I always knew...

MA: It only happened once. Once... Once was all it took.

A stunned silence. Even JAKE wasn't prepared for this.

Then the very next day, your Da decides to "service me" he says. He could be so coarse. So when it happened, I didn't know what to think.

JAKE: (*It sinks in.*) Uncle Dick?

MA: I didn't think it was possible. I thought it was only cats. Then I read in the paper – about a woman who'd had twins by different fathers.

JAKE: Uncle Dick was my Da?

MA: Not you! Charlie! Charlie was Dick's boy! (*Breaks down.*) I'm sorry. I tried, Charlie, I really tried... (*Crawls toward CHARLES, sobbing.*)

CHARLES: No. No. No! Stop it! Both of you. Don't you see? You just feed each other's delusions.

JAKE: Denial, Charles, is not a river in –

CHARLES: We're twins, Jake! Alright, call it a half-truth – God knows it's the best we can hope for in this family! Let's say she did have her little fling with Uncle Dick, that it all happened like she says – what does it prove? Did we have tests? No! You can't know that, Ma.

MA: A mother always knows.

CHARLES: Most mothers don't need to know! So... You slept with two brothers, then found you were pregnant – God! I'm not blaming you, Ma, it must have been terrible, especially in those days – no-one to talk to. And the guilt and the shame and the doubt... And the thought preys on your mind. Who's the father?

JAKE: You sound like my therapist!

CHARLES: (*Ignoring him, to MA.*) Until something has to give and you suddenly hit on a breathtakingly simple solution. You split us, fifty-fifty.

JAKE: Two seeds. "Two nations in thy womb", Ma. Jacob and Esau. See, Charlie? They switched the names to fool us.

CHARLES: Yes, wouldn't it be nice if we could all agree on a nice tidy little myth to explain it all away. Maybe we should've been identical – (*To MA.*) Then at least you'd've known we were both Da's or –

MA: That's the trouble, Charlie. He was more identical than you.

CHARLES: Then you really could've treated us *exactly* the same. Then maybe Jake would've been allowed to be ordinary and I could've let my hair down once in a while instead of always having to be Sensible Charles! Don't you see, Ma, what you're saying, it's... monstrous.

MA: The truth always is.

She crouches over her books, gathering them up in her arms.

CHARLES: Well no I'm sorry, Ma, but the really monstrous truth is that you never get to the bottom of it – why sometimes it all goes horribly wrong for no apparent reason, not enough love, or too much, the wrong kind, the kind of love no son can possibly deserve, or ever repay. Maybe *that's* Jake's problem. Ma? Where you going? Ma!

MA scuttles out to the hall, clutching her remaining books.

JAKE: Now look what you've done.

CHARLES: I'm sorry, Jake, but I won't allow you to –

JAKE: Allow me? Hear that, Claudette! I'm not allowed to solve my own riddles! That's our Charles! The conscientious carer. Always so solicitous, so bloody – what's the word, Da?

CHARLES: You don't mean that.

JAKE: Unctuous. Unctuous.

CHARLES: I'm trying to help!

JAKE: You're worse than Ma! (*CHARLES stares at him, stunned.*) Ever wonder why you're so keen to sort out my problems?

CHARLES: Oh, something else you'd like to share with us?

JAKE: What's your problem, Charlie? What's left to deny?

CHARLES: What else can you dig up? Uncle Dick? You've already got Da whacking him on the head with his spade. Now you've got your motive. Go ahead! Reopen the inquest! Dig 'em all up! Rattle their bones till they tell you what you want to hear! D'you think that'll solve anything?

JAKE: Indeed I do! (*To CLAUDETTE, milking the courtroom drama.*) I put it to you, m'lud, that the key to the mystery lies – in this 'ere Book. (*Brandishes the book.*) Question is, m'lud, whence do these mysterious messages arise?

CHARLES: I told you. He has the old girl up all night scribbling.

JAKE: My Father's Ghost? Come on, Charlie! You don't seriously expect me to believe all this – table-knocking and talking in tongues? I may be mad but I'm not stupid. I'm not denying that's Ma's handwriting, but those are Da's words – I'd know them anywhere, in any hand. (*To CLAUDETTE.*) I put it to you, m'lud, that if quid pro quo and sine qua non aforesaid messages come straight from the horse's mouth, if you'll pardon our predeliction for barnyard metaphors –

CHARLES: (*To CLAUDETTE.*) See what happens when he stops taking his tablets?

JAKE: Then it follows ipso facto that m'learned friend's objection – (*Indicates CHARLES.*) derives entirely –

CHARLES: I did try to warn you!

JAKE: From aforesaid horse's t'other end!

CLAUDETTE: (*Smiles, humouring him.*) It's alright, Jake.

JAKE: No, m'lud. If this stuff is coming direct from our Da then it can only mean that – (*Ambushed by his own logic, to CHARLES.*) Da isn't dead! You and Ma are keeping him alive, force-feeding him, plugging him into the old voice-box. You've got him hidden away in the – (*Flash of insight.*) The cupboard!

He runs to the cupboard, rattling the padlocked door.

CHARLES: Jake! Don't be ridicul...

JAKE: I bet you even signed the death certificate. (*Heads for the scullery.*)

CHARLES: Jake? Where are you –

JAKE: Or got one of your creepy doctor friends to do the dirty. (*Runs off.*)

CHARLES: (*Shouting after him.*) You're nuts!

JAKE: (*Shouting, off.*) So you all keep telling me!

CHARLES: (*Shouting back.*) Jake! Listen. All it takes is one tablet –

From the scullery: crashing and clattering noises. Smoke wafts in from the hall.

(*To CLAUDETTE.*) I really am most terribly sorry. Look, erm... Would you mind calling an ambulance?

CLAUDETTE: (*Picks up the phone, dials 999.*) What about the police?

CHARLES: What about – No! Not the police! This is a private matter.

JAKE reappears from the scullery, clutching a spade.

Erm... Take it easy, Jake...

CLAUDETTE: (*Sniffs the air.*) Er... Maybe I should call the fire brigade.

CHARLES: (*Follows her gaze, seeing the smoke.*) Oh no. Ma. Ma!

He runs off, left. JAKE stares blankly at CLAUDETTE.

JAKE: Oh... Hullo, Claudette.

CLAUDETTE carefully replaces the receiver. An awkward, dangerous silence.

Look, I... I hope this won't affect the plans for the wedding.

CLAUDETTE: (*Laughs nervously.*) Er... No... Why should it?

JAKE: You didn't like the caviar? (*Stares mournfully at the untouched plate.*) The funeral bak'd meats...

CLAUDETTE: (*Glancing at her watch.*) God! Is that the time? I must dash – got a client tomorrow morning – nine thirty – (*Grabs her coat.*) I'll call you, Jake –

JAKE: (*Involuntarily rasing the spade.*) No! Claudette...
Don't go.

CHARLES leads MA in from the hall coughing and spluttering. Her hair is singed, her face smeared with soot.

CHARLES: (*To JAKE.*) Her bedroom's on fire. She tried to burn the books.

MA: I'll burn it down before I let her get her grasping little –

JAKE: Claudette!

CLAUDETTE takes advantage of the distraction to run off through the scullery, leaving JAKE silently gesturing after her.

CHARLES: (*Leading MA by the arm.*) Come on, Ma...
This way.

MA: (*Clutching his arm.*) Da! He's still in there!

CHARLES: Da's dead.

MA: He'll be burnt alive!

CHARLES: (*Gently.*) He's dead, Ma. Dead and buried.
This is us grieving.

MA: (*Another rush of panic.*) Jake!

CHARLES: I'll come back for him.

MA: (*Gripping him tightly.*) No! No, Charles, I don't want to lose you both!

CHARLES: (*Patiently.*) This way, Ma.

He leads her off through the scullery, leaving JAKE alone.

Noises off: crackling flames. Smoke thickens. The kitchen is suffused in a red glow. JAKE wields the spade, smashing the padlock from the cupboard door.

The door swings open to reveal: a shrine: candles and fairy lights; old photographs and relics of Da; his empty wheelchair with the built-in voice-box, lit by the phosphorescent glow of the computer screen.

JAKE: Da... Da... Speak to me, Da? I'm sorry, Da... I honestly didn't come home to cause trouble. Then again, as Ma would say, it's things like this bring the family together. Together. You and me, Da. What do you say? Hunting and gathering like in the old days. Da? Go on, you old bugger, say something! You're supposed to tell me the meaning of life.

Sounds of the house burning down, subsumed in heavenly music as DA's machine-voice crackles from within the shrine.

DA: Together... to gather... to go...
   Forgive them... Jake....
   For what cannot be undone...
   Heal thy Ma...
   Thy brother Cain and thy brother Jacob...
   Heal them...
   For I am not a God of Vengeance...
   And thou art my son... Esau... In whom I am...
   Listen... Listen to thy dead Da talking...
   Forgive them Jake...
   Forgive them... for... they... know... not... what... they... do...

JAKE stares at the shrine, transfixed. Music. Red light fades to blackout.

The End